who wants to create Australia?

Essays on poetry and ideas in contemporary Australia

Martin Harrison

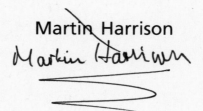

HALSTEAD PRESS

contents

introduction

One of the main reasons for writing about poetry is to share the pleasure of reading it. A further pleasure and a further motive are to deepen one's understanding of the vitality of poetry as a contemporary art-form. These are thoughts I had in mind in bringing these essays together in a single book.

Some of the pieces which follow are accounts of particular readings of contemporary poets and poems. To a degree they form a fairly arbitrary portrait of some of the contemporary work I enjoy reading and thinking about: many other contemporary Australian poems and poets that I admire are not mentioned in this book. But these essays account for at least some of the poems in which a creative convergence of poem and idea seemed necessary and natural on my first encounter with them. Momentarily it became essential to think through the experience of the poem and speculate with it, tracing out its setting and its many-sidedness. At the same time these are poems which have signposted for me key features of the local environs of a contemporary Australian poetry. Whatever might be said of them in terms of how they register certain persistent concerns – to do with modernity and the end of modernity, with post-colonialism. place and globalism, or with our recent worldly anxieties about selfhood and its meaning – they are also poems which have worked on me in a much more direct sense than any critical terms could easily convey.

A few of these essays have a more exploratory purpose about clarifying the nature of the poet's work and the nature of the poem. What is poetry now? What sort of experience does it bring forward? How does the work of the poet connect with other art forms and other ideas about writing? These were often background questions I was thinking about while writing. Ours is a period, after all, in which influential ideas about language and writing have sought to dislodge poetry from a central position in modern literature. At the same time, the activity of understanding a poem – in particular what sort of sensory experience it conveys and what sort of information it can gather – has necessarily become involved in a dialogue with shifting concepts of idea and image, with other media and with other experiences of performance. Of course, the long-lived record of innovation and experiment in modernist and post-modernist poetry demonstrates that this dialogue has been going on for many decades. But this seems to be a time of particularly intense convergence between often contradictory ideas about language, medium and experience and their connection with poetry.

Far from the discussion of poetry opening up towards these zones of art, technology, performance and philosophy so closely allied to it, it seems that there is also a real danger in our time – not just in Australia, I must add – that talk of poetry becomes a

who wants to create Australia?

narrow kind of talk, exclusive of poetry readers' other interests and experiences. This sense that somehow critical discussion of poetry is removed from the mainstream or increasingly irrelevant to it is part of a larger picture in which all literary criticism has suffered from what one Australian critic, some thirty years ago, presciently termed its "over-efficiency": its professionalisation, its far too clever intellectual skill, its lack of surprise.[1] Often, too, criticism looks arcane to an outsider not because there is some legitimately complex issue of scholarship, but for quite trivial and trivialising intellectual reasons. Literary "in-house" matters, the deadly process of respectabilisation-by-theory, the reduction of poetry to a cliché useful for nation-building, the dogmas of poetic controversy: all in their different ways turn poetry into a vehicle whose wheels grind downwards in the sand.

Reasonably enough, readers give up reading poetry when they feel that poems can no longer address the significant big and the significant small questions of their lives. Those questions may be the formative ones concerning language, medium and meaning. Or they may be more intuitive and, in a sense, more everyday; in other words, issues to do with emotion whether pain or pleasure, or to do with deep and ultimately moral matters in the experience of living and dying. But readers also give up if, under much more deeply dispersed pressures, poetry just stops looking like a part of the instrument panel, if it stops looking like a lively, challenging, emotionally fresh and intelligent part of the repertoire of activities which construct an engagement with contemporary experience and meaning. In a climate where poetry is made to look both hostile and dull, the activity of reading and the poet's voice drift apart from each other like two people walking down opposite shores of an ever widening river entrance.

So it is a tall order indeed that a group of essays comprehend the exigencies of a forthright, occasionally complex discussion of ideas plus an engagement with ductile, hard-to-define issues concerning voice and experience in the exploration of poetry as a practice. I see no other way, however, to talk about poetry if it is to be represented as a primary and meaningful art form for today. That has been one of the ideals in bring-ing these pieces together. At best, all they can do is make a contribution to what is the perennial readerly and critical discussion of poetry going on in reviews, other publications, private letters, electronic lists, readings, conversations in and outside the class room or seminar and just plain, everyday talk.

If they make some contribution to the excitement of contemporary Australian poetry, I have to thank a number of readers, many of them poets, who have given me confidence that I was not totally off-beam in what I was saying, in particular Peter Minter, Robert Adamson, Judith Beveridge, John Mateer, Jill Jones and Robert Gray who have all offered useful suggestions at various stages of the writing. Many people – too many people to mention here – have been part of the discussions and conversations about poetry which have been the seedbed of these ideas. I have been lucky enough to carry on this discussion about poetry whether in talks at festivals, in seminars with young poets, in talking with students and in correspondence with friends and fellow writers. I sincerely thank too the editors of the journals *Australian Book Review, Boxkite, Five Bells, Heat, Meanjin, Southerly, Ulitarra* and *Text* where a number of these essays

---

1 H.P. Heseltine, "Criticism and the Individual Talent," in ed.Delys Bird, Robert Dixon and Christopher Lee, *Authority and Influence: Australian Literary Criticism 1950 – 2000*, University of Queensland Press, Brisbane, 2001, p 74

appeared in earlier, often substantially different, versions. My publishers Neil James and Matthew Richardson looked out for this collection sooner than I was able to deliver it and their care and patience have been beyond the call of duty. Finally, had it not been for the tenacity and sharpness of critic and editor, the late Helen Daniel, who published more than a number of reviews and notes of mine in *Australian Book Review* I might easily have thought such a book was not worth attempting.

1

The end of linear writing is indeed
the end of the book.

Jacques Derrida

who wants to create Australia?

Sometime in the early 90s I was invited down to Melbourne to give a talk. An all day session of writers and artists was scheduled as part of a larger event where economists, cultural theorists, political scientists all had their days too. The brief was to talk about the future of Australia and in particular new ideas, new trends, new practices. There was much talk in political circles at the time about the importance of innovation and the artist's contribution. Much in the spirit of the time, the invitation from the organisers had been enthusiastic in its outline of what the three or four days would encompass, not least the importance of what writers and artists had to say in the larger national debate. The event, staged before a sizeable professional and general audience in downtown Melbourne, was about thinking the future creatively. Like an advice-giving session or a brainstorming session, the panels and talks would function as a stimulus or guide for future policy. It would tell us something about where the country was heading. I was not sure what contribution my ideas could make but I flew to Melbourne with some sense of expectation, making corrections to the the talk I had prepared for the allotted half hour time slot.

I wanted to talk about literature and visual art or more exactly about the way in which key ideas about Australian culture were framed in terms of specific types of literary and artistic work. Yet (I wanted to add) it was self evident that there had been a movement among critics, and many writers and artists, to re-think the nature of art in relation to contemporary technologies, especially digital and cinematic technologies. This exciting contemporary moment was one in which the more innovative artists and writers were shifting their work away from the traditional and classical forms of writing and art-making, away, that is, from forms such as the poem, the novel, the painting, the singular object-based sculpture, scripted live theatre and so on.

And the questions or issues which I hoped this brief talk might introduce? They were about how or whether such new forms of work could continue to maintain the connection between art and nation which the older forms had often relied on, refining ideas of self and awareness within local representations of people, land, landscape and country. Would the assumption that the idea of place and identity, on the one hand, and the practice of literature and painting, on the other, had a natural closeness to each other continue to make sense? And more to the point: did this assumption about the connection between art and nation transfer to video art, installation art, interactive works, discontinuous narratives, sound works and so on? In some measure, then, it was a talk drawn from criticism and critical theory, including the poetics of the image and of the object and their associated historical and cultural contexts.

It is not too suprising that this was so. I was immersed at the time in the ideas of writers, historians, art critics and media critics who stressed a literariness in our understanding of Australia, a literariness which though still connected with the poem or novel was of a more foundational sort. A new wave of critical writing was appearing, for instance, which not only explored Australian settlement as a chronological record in a social historical way but explored the texts, the writing and, as it were, the thought systems at work in white settlement – and then extended these ideas to the consequent later developments and changes in landscape, in the built environment, in social relations and in matters to do with race. To use the parlance of the time, these things were also "readable" texts.

To take one example: Paul Carter, probably with the issue of Indigenous perceptions of country and invasion especially in mind, was writing about "spatial history" and how the spatial history he looked forward to, a history which reflected on sensory perception and the environment, would be a history which offered only one self re-flective account among a variety of versions. Spatial history stood, as he put it, in a "metaphorical" relationship to the writing of Indigenous writers who were also telling their story and describing their sense of place. Such a history, he went on, in *The Road to Botany Bay*,

> would be a comparable reflection on different historical content.
> And naturally since the medium of white history is writing, [a spatial history] would not simply be a book about the history of recollection. Such a history, giving back to metaphor its ontological role and recovering its historical space, would inevitably and properly be a poetic history.[2]

With all such claims I felt a certain unease about whether the theoretical project they offered could properly accommodate the sense of immediate, recountable experiences in everyday life both now and in the past. Yet it was clear that questions how – and by whom – land and landscape are thought and written, how social experience is documented and what sort of psychological geography is formed as part of the "modern" invention of Australia were being treated in a complex, inclusive and self reflective way.

It was clear too that no straightforward identification could be made between art, identity and history writing as if they all said the same thing or pointed in the same direction. The tracings of connection, disconnection and silence in Australian language and culture could, for instance, be mapped in the status of traditional languages and cultures as perceived by white Australia in the 19th century through to a host of cross-cultural and bi-cultural historical encounters that occurred in the 20th century and which are only now being acknowledged historically and legally. Likewise, the liveliness of these issues to do with representation, thought and place was (and still is) to be found in the visual tradition of much recent Australian art-making. This is particularly so when we consciously identify and contrast the way in which European techniques of landscape painting and the picturesque relate to their more modern correlative of "land." Or when we understand the effect on our sense of country of the imposition of Western notions of surveying and enclosure within optical space. Ten or more years ago there was, and perhaps there still is, a lively debate about how older 19th century views and practices obviously contrast with a latterday, arguably belated under-

---

2 Paul Carter, *The Road to Botany Bay: An Essay in Spatial History*, Faber and Faber, London, 1987, p 350

standing of traditional Aboriginal graphic and performative systems. They contrast also with the obvious impact of cinematic and photographic ways of representing place and space in modernist and post-modernist art and literature. Again the ideas of writers like Paul Carter and the film-maker and critic Ross Gibson were partly at the back of my mind in making these connections.

No doubt, too, a lot more could have been said that day about the way in which visual technologies change the way stories are told and written. Some of these changes were briefly touched on in the talk I was planning for Melbourne. They go back to the idea sketched above: do art objects which are composed largely within the field of new media technologies closely relate to larger narratives of the "meaning" or "significance" of a local culture? For the ethnographer and theorist Eric Michaels (whom I was also reading at the time) it was the making of narrative itself and, in a specialist way, the very task of "making sense" through narrative which the new media and particularly mass media like television were beginning to undermine. I had marked a particular quote to do with what he called the capacity to "play with the responsibility to mean" which, he argued, is opened up in post-modern televisual format. Back in 1987 he had written about the impact of television and the video clip:

> something starts happening in which the literary bias of narrative is exploded and we get stories that exploit, rather than resist, the divorce of signifier and signified, image and narrative meaning, which moving picture (film or video) technology permits. Commercial television [has] had a great influence here, because the effect of its economic rationale on the narrative format/sequence [is] profound. The insertion of irrelevant bits of advertising into the program narrative has [...] trained two generations of viewers to accept the deconstructive possibilities of audiovisual sequencing.[3]

This theme to do with how technologies of seeing and hearing influence the ways in which we conceive objects and information and the differences between technological realisation and literary writing is one which fascinates me. As Michaels envisaged, new epistemologies emerge with new techniques. What we see is not only about "seeing" in a narrow optical sense but about how meaning links up with sensory experiences in broader and often unconsciously registered ways. These new ways of responding and seeing start to look natural when they occur in media practice and soon they beome naturalised within various visual art practices or in what writers do in novels, drama and poems. More, under the pressure of new technologies writers and artists have long ago started to move out of traditional media such as the print book or the canvas painting to work with the image and meaning systems of other technologies; while traditionally conceived and presented art works and literature borrow structural features from, and make references to, the way that the world is viewed and imagined through electronic media. Some version of this was what I was going to say.

It was clear to me, however, that there were other aspects of communication technologies and media which posed difficult and disturbing challenges to our definition of terms such as "object" and "meaning". The quote from Eric Michaels briefly touched on this aspect of new technologies with its reference to the "deconstructive possibilities" of audiovisual works and the suggestion that there is a "divorce" bet-

---

3 Eric Michaels, *Bad Aboriginal Art: Tradition, Media and Technological Horizon*, Allen and Unwin, Sydney, 1994, p 177

ween surface features of the text or image and the signified levels of meaning. One problem, for instance, I wanted to pose in the context of a debate about future directions was the difficulty which technological means and technicised artefacts pose when it comes to finding adequate descriptions for them critically and aesthetically. In their mass form, such artefacts (television programs, for instance) and their means of production are usually not uniquely authored; usually they lack distinguishing hand-made traits and individual signatures; and many times they are not even stable and long-lived objects. Viewers and readers rapidly (often unreflectively yet not un-intelligently) "consume" them. Sustained, self aware viewing and reading are not what they propose.

Electronic media pose problems too when it comes to defining their location in the sense of their attachment to region and their local symbolic significance within, for example, contexts such as the idea of "Australia" or "Australian", so much so that issues to do with a media item's national origin or its connection with the defining of national identity start to look tenuous and irrelevant. Like the satellite footprint which does not literally make a foot-shaped declivity in the land the artefacts associated with information technologies (TV series, logos, fashion designs, popular music styles, mass-produced news images and so on) are often only momentarily stabilised effects and accordingly they are indiscriminate, not tied down in language and place. Yet they have extraordinary psychological impacts. They orient whole rifts of cultural view and opinion.

Similarly, the talk I planned could not help but refer to an already very present sense of worldwide communication systems. It was clear, for instance, that the symbolic community collectives which were starting to assemble around newer forms of digital communication systems (websites, databases, worldwide e-mail, worldwide news systems) spoke outside of or, more accurately, on the other side of any singular, national or Australian idiom. Not unlike the international finance systems which are so closely allied to them, these systems stress transfer, contact, lack of physical substance, the limitlessness of memories, the replacement of conceptual territories ("I have just been talking to Tokyo") and most importantly transportability from place to place, from text to image, from image to image. At the very least one of the issues which these and similar communicative means, means which neither chisel nor literalise, were starting to involve us in was the pressing question of whether contemporary culture must now be thought of as mainly an act of recovery and preservation. The view I wanted to discuss was the view which says: Cultural artefacts like poems, novels, plays and paintings cannot now escape their nostalgic, out-of-date technical format and most of what contemporary artists do is, at heart, an activity whose main value is to breathe new life into dead forms such as the novel and theatre. This is the view which says that current art practice reduces art to being a representational medium in which increasingly sophisticated and innovative ways are invented to conserve, re-circulate and re-present the art and writing of the past. In the hi-tech context, art and literature are the freshly minted exhibits in a digital museum. Ten years ago it was certainly possible to start thinking, albeit metaphorically, that the stable cultural streetscape of great art works including electronic ones like films and TV, and the cultural history surrounding them, were disintegrating into a system of movement and transfer which had to be permanently repaired and reorganised, much like the freeways and parking lots of an anonymous Los Angeles. Or an increasingly anonymous, internationalised and "global" (as the pundits would now have it) Australia.

At the same time I had no desire to welcome the future in a state of dumb acquiescence. I was already feeling unhappy with the way theorists were suggesting an approach to art-making puritanically tied to new technologies, an approach subservient to a philosophical view of art which stresses the absence or disintegration of permanent and permanently meaningful structures. Far from leading through to pieces elegantly and economically conceived in media format, my concern was that a makeshift and impoverished art would occur, an art which lacked resonance and memorability. Where writing was concerned there was the risk that far from leading to new directions which respond both to innovative technical form and to different orders of perception, a surrogate form of literature was being produced where differences between writers disappeared in a broadly based activity of "textuality", a practice of writing beyond recognisable genre, of writing for expression alone, of writing according to a formula, whether dictated by an experimental procedure or by the commercial requirements of niche marketing. It was clear that the new commercial and technological contexts for writing were already leaving us without many powerful novels or significant books of poems. Much new work (which, as the hype machine geared up, was backed by huge publicity campaigns and even appeared in so-called quality journals) struck me as indeed just "writing".

As we now know, the 90s would be a period where fake reputations exploded on the fiction, visual art and poetry scenes. Of course where the later development of the internet and websites are concerned, this parallel sense of both flatness and pretentiousness may be no more than the result of a few self-announcing writers, mostly poets, scattering far and wide their meaningless confetti. Off or on the web, everyone has learnt that without editors, critics, critical exchange and debate, the work – the writing – risks turning out to be little more than written "chat" ballooning up behind inflated names.

***

I never gave the talk. Between getting on the plane and making contact with the organisers a day or so later, the event went through a re-organisation or, as we now call it, a "re-structuring". Somehow the economists could not be fitted into their allotted time, and everybody else had to move place and reduce their participation. There was indeed a large contingent of experts in economics, nearly all of whom (as I remember) had the same thing to say, largely consisting in variations on the theme of "We don't know". Speaker after speaker, economics academics, government administrators, think-tank researchers and consultants fed out the line that there were no underlying theories behind economic study worth supporting, that economists just studied trends and financial phenomena, that little could be predicted ahead of time and that the market did more or less what it liked. Most people, I suspect, have long grown inured to this mix of professionalised pragmatics, indifference and economic weather watching. Across the planet they are what characterise a period where the very rich have benefitted massively at the expense of the poor.

In the event's re-shaping, the political scientists and the cultural studies people definitely fared better timewise than the artists, film-makers and writers. There were even a couple of lengthy talks. From this distance (and quite probably at the time) I cannot remember a word that was said. The high-flying academics mouthed polite and complimentary things about the Labor Party and took pains with their papers to reference a number of widely published colleagues and a few so-called public intellectuals, most of whom were sitting in the audience. But the opportunity of a day-long discussion with artists and writers was reduced to a single session on the final morning where approximately twelve or so people were asked if they would mind limiting their prepared contributions to what immediately comes to mind as the most banal thing you can associate with the word "artist". Could we limit our contributions to an artist's *statement*? Five minutes long, ideally. Somehow the insanely arrogant slogan of "creating Australia" (through art, presumably) got attached to the session. We all trooped up on to the stage. It was how I imagine one of those TV quiz shows where lots of contestants have a few seconds to speak on camera. Only there were no cameras.

It was clear that the interlinked themes which I had prepared to talk about – to do with literature, place and displacement, to do with the potentially displacing impact of electronic artefacts and to do with the impact of digital systems – would have to wait for another time. It was a pity: the intention behind the event had been a worthwhile one. On the other hand, much of the cultural experience I wanted to discuss was so recent, relatively speaking, that I wonder how useful my talk would have been. Time has made it easier to appreciate the complexity of the ways in which writing and creative practice respond to the re-ordering of custom and opinion and to issues like the re-siting of information systems in contemporary technologies and the new effects and narratives of TV, film and popular media. In saying that, there is no suggestion that what is problematic about the idea of a contemporary writing or art practice has somehow gone away. But clearly I was trying to make connections some of which may not have been as obvious as they are now. Others may just have been false trails.

By the same token, the mists of rhetoric which surrounded the web have largely been dispelled. As many knew at the time, a shift in the information interface *has* constituted a shift in communication practices and, to some extent, in creative practices. And there *are* further ramifications in terms of how individuals think of themselves as communicators and how our sensory awareness is both unconsciously and consciously influenced by new media, being both heightened and de-sensitised in the process. There is much greater clarity, too, in critical discourse and artistic debate about the issues of craft, métier, construction and long-term durability of works of art and writing than there was back then. The literary scandals of the 90s have hopefully acted as a reminder that questions of authority and authorship cannot be facilely brushed aside. On the other hand, it is arguable that no period in Australia's post-Federation cultural history has been so subsumed in overseas influences as our "Americanised" contemporary culture is. The language of nation, too, is as troubled and obfuscatory as it ever was. Recent events like the scapegoating of refugees and immigrants as potential terrorists, for example, constitute degrading appeals to the electorate in the name of "nation" and so-called "community;" but they do not hide the fact that the questions to do with writing about, and understanding, a many-voiced Australian history await a much more far-sighted and ethically conscious intellectual leadership than the country has at present. The subtle, deep questions of what is meant by a literature or a poetics in Australia have not gone away.

In the statement I finally read there was no opportunity, likewise, to draw attention to two other quotations. The first was from the critic and editor Harry Heseltine writing about what he unhesitatingly called Australian culture in a 1962 essay in the magazine *Meanjin*. Heseltine felt obliged to repeat what he felt was still a key question asked by Australians about their culture: Is it enough? Or paraphrased: Is the storehouse of local culture, is what comes to hand as work from and about the culture, sufficient as a representation of a nation? Today this question appears archaic, even embarrassing. In 1962 it was:

> the question students of Australian culture are driven to again and again. Is our tradition, after all, to be summed up in this or that single world – Mateship? Landscape? Nationalism? Is what we have received from our literary past so *thin* that the simple labels do, in fact, suffice? Most of us would find it difficult to believe that the literature of any nation could be reduced to such direct and formulary clarity...[4]

Whilst accepting the final qualification, my purpose in quoting this was to put a historical marker in the sand. But it was also to ask whether, on reflection, Heseltine's questions and his concern about reductiveness were that bad. Provided they can be asked in a way which is not demoralising or cringing, versions of these questions perhaps should continue to be asked from time to time. Heseltine asked them within reach of a period in which some of the most powerful literary and artistic work ever made in this country was being produced – including the work of the Heide group and the Antipodeans and such writers as Patrick White, Judith Wright, Francis Webb and David Campbell. The questions are about not simplifying, not narrowing, the thematic range of contemporary work just as much as they are about what may have seemed at the time a lack of a moment of cultural emergence.

This is where the other quotation had some relevance. It is a one-liner from the poet James McAuley:

> there is no genuine poetry which corresponds to the "modernity" present in our heritage.[5]

Apart from turning us specifically to poetry, this quote was also meant as a marker, not so much of time but rather of the endpoint of a polemic. For McAuley's definition of modernity (first given in a lecture in 1955) is eccentric and extravagantly large-scale even by the Cold War standards of the time. Historically, "modernity" meant to McAuley most if not all of what we call the Enlightenment: localised to his own times, this argumentatively defined "modernity" includes a grab-bag of mainly intellectual hatreds supposedly derived from the Enlightenment and which range from any and all non-Christian philosophy through to what McAuley sees as the far Left in politics. Rather suprisingly, into this jumble he tosses his own simplifying version of a white, monocultural, securely parliamentary, union-free, politically unrancorous, incorruptible, liberal-thinking mainstream Australian history. Thank goodness, McAuley goes on, despite all this progressivism we are not too far-gone in "modernity" and still

4 H.P. Heseltine, "The Australian Image: The Literary Heritage", *Meanjin*, 1,1962, reprinted in ed. Clement Semmler, *Twentieth Century Australian Literary Criticism*, Oxford University Press, Melbourne, 1967, p 89

5 James McAuley, *The End of Modernity: Essays on Literature, Art and Culture*, Angus and Robertson, Sydney, 1959, p 63

have enough Christian residues in our culture to ensure that our heritage is "reassuringly old-fashioned".

My motive in quoting this was to signal how different, how much more subtle and deeply researched an understanding of modernity was required; and in particular how the poet's dated Cold War rhetoric looked severely squewed within a couple of years of the Berlin Wall's demolition. In fairness, McAuley himself seems to have understood the problem at the heart of his polemic for in a later essay he writes of how, like it or not, we *"cannot* act as if the intense experiences of the last one hundred and fifty years had never been; we *cannot* suppress and deny the voices of that period [i.e. 150 years of "modernity"] that continue to speak in us."[6] The problem was that his narrowly anti-modern platform was too controversial, too doggedly political and intellectualistic even for him. Besides, how sensibly did his tirade tie into the matter of writing poetry? That 150 years of post-Enlightenment culture of Romanticism and modernism corresponds to nearly the entire colonial and modern period of Australian art and writing, let alone the modern period of poetry in French or Spanish or German (some of the latter of which McAuley would later translate brilliantly.)

My comment, then, would obviously have been about history, about recognising that the experience offered in art is an always contemporary experience, constructed in its own time by significant artists and writers. It would also have been about technology and about poetic creation. Partly it would have been about cutting through false, prevaricating, culturally single strand, more or less racist views about Australian modernity and would have asserted the capacity of poets, writers and artists to confront and understand their contemporary world. Or perhaps that is a comment added in hindsight. As I look back to that day in Melbourne, it would have come as a surprise to think that a new version of those same reassuringly old-fashioned, falsely comforting, mainstream views would momentarily emerge over the decade to come, as if anyone could somehow overlook the manipulation and untruthfulness behind them. As if somehow we could overlook the children floating in the ocean.

---

6 James McAuley, op cit, p 159. Italics added.

2

Poetry differs from all her sisters in this one important respect, that...consciousness is also the actual material in which she works. Consciousness is to her what their various mediums (marble, pigments etc) are to the other arts.

Owen Barfield

the tenth muse [7]

*H*er words often come back to me when I think about teaching poetry. She was not the first person to express such an opinion, but the tiredness and clarity with which this elderly, world-travelled woman expressed herself was unforgettable: "It is impossible to teach someone to become a poet." She was a relative I acquired through marriage in the years I lived in New Zealand during the 70s. Her existence had been a rumour till I went to live there. As fate would have it, she is also the only person I have ever met who knew D.H. Lawrence in person. Inevitably there were anecdotes and lovely stories to listen to, some about Lawrence's banned painting exhibition, a few about his life in the USA. There was another side to her past life too: she had at one point in the 1920s worked for Chanel. Here – but it was not just the passage of time which made her reticent – she was less forthcoming: the life of a successful Parisian model and cocaine addiction were themes closely associated in her memories of the time back then. I had not realised such an addiction existed back then, so early on in the last century. I still had much to learn about the secret histories and inheritances of the past.

Of course like all young writers I found a lot of these secret histories already inside me. But many of them were adduced, were brought to the light, by a group of people, like the elderly English woman living in Auckland, upon whose lives I haphazardly chanced. It is probably a common enough experience when you are young. In my case, the people I am thinking about are all largely unknown. Mostly by the time I met them they were living retired lives in quiet suburban houses crammed with letters, books and pictures. If I run through them as a list in my own mind, they make up a rather bizarre group – a retired travel agent, an expatriate American psychoanalyst, a wealthy German emigré, an Iranian exile, an elderly world-travelling Swedish woman, two aged Jewish scholars, the long-neglected child of a famous modernist poet, the mother of a writer who had died years before of a tragic illness.

The list could go on. I met a lot of such people in my early years; one day I will perhaps feel able to fully honour their influence and write about them in detail. They are the people often unacknowledged in biographies largely because their presence is fleeting. They are the people who open up their art collections, their translations, their houses, their previous reading and, most important of all, their memories to a potential forthcoming writer. Sometimes they had been there in the painter's studio, on the set, at the meeting; or they had been the backers, the publishers or the rescuers of some of those whom we now think of as major figures.

Most importantly they were the people who carried the temper of their times, being

---

7 First published in *Text*, 1/1 (1997)

who wants to create Australia?

still able to give you the street-detail, the angle of the light on a particular day. Just as crucial as the work or the idea, they provided the mood or atmosphere in which the work or the idea were achieved. They were able to pass on the hidden detail; they were the ones who opened up windows on a past not found in books. Perhaps most valuably, they dispelled much of the idolatry with which art-practice and the artist's life are regarded these days (especially in the media) and reported instead on an existence which was local, human, domestic. Almost inadvertently they are the people who show how so much which seems new to the new artist or new writer is in fact no more than his or her period's repetition of themes, ambitions and life-styles long gone. They show how, despite difference of age, place and circumstances, we are making much the same attempt.

Over a hundred years ago, André Gide celebrated this aspect of writing as a kind of encounter, as the ability to maintain your imaginative life in a state of permanent openness and discovery. The gift of the poet, he makes the poet-teacher figure Ménalque say in *Fruits of the Earth,* is the gift of encounter, of meeting.[8] This gift brings you people, things, experiences, emotions. It brings you to them. Gide's comment is not without a slight trace of qualification: Ménalque's life has itself been exuberant but troubled. Of course, we have all seen young writers who have this gift in excess, or who are too impatient to understand it or who lack it or who, worse, substitute for it a frenzy of literary friendships and literary politics. There are writers too who will be denied this gift by circumstances beyond their control, by an unpredictable future or a hostile environment. Things quite simply do not work out as they should or could. A poet is no more free of the *guignol* than anyone else: ill health, crippling anxiety, unceasing external demands, poverty of mind and spirit, poverty in the savings account will stop you in your tracks. Who, for instance, can cope with what most writers are condemned to in the form of ever-present financial anxiety and job insecurity?

So the words of an elderly relative who died nearly twenty years ago recur when I think about teaching poetry. To remember them is partly a way of reminding myself of self evident truths to do with sources of information, with influences and friendships – mainly, that if these factors bode well, then you teach yourself what you need to know. Partly, however, I remember them because they also state some basic facts to do with the way that any young writer acquires for better or worse that world-sense or worldly sense by which an art or craft is indelibly marked. It is a question, in other words, of getting wisdom whatever its sources may be. Such knowledge always arrives in a way which is appropriate to you and maybe not to anyone else. In this sense, all writing is handed on. It is not taught.

2

Many other aspects of reading and writing, however, are taught. Older humanist styles of critical reading, those styles of reading which are about response, scholarship and evaluation, took it for granted that literature and in particular poetry were the primary objects of its attention. Humanist values were the values of imagination, of emotional engagement. Reading had to do with the assessment of tonality, of craft and

---

8 André Gide, *Les nourritures terrestres, Gallimard: Livre de Poche*, Paris 1971, p 69. "Don du poète, m'écriais-je, tu es le don de perpétuelle rencontre."

feeling, together with all the matters which adjoin them to the life experience or views of the writer. Partly deriving from classical and biblical scholarship, this sort of criticism also borrowed many of its terms directly from the practices of creative writers. There was so close a symbiosis between the two practices that the recreative critical reading of poetry was often initially taught (in universities, for instance) as the foundation practice for sophisticated critical reading – and then extended out to other sorts of writing. While it would be an exaggeration to say that such practices have totally disappeared, they long ago ceased to be central practices in the study of literature. The problem is even worse than mere decay or disappearance, for that at least would allow for a clean break and a new start. Evacuated, the terms of humanist reading are still on the scene, popularised as authenticity, intimacy and the personal voice of the writer. They have become more or less the argot of the book publisher's marketing campaign.

Responsive, self conscious critical reading may have lost its importance, but criticism and poetics certainly have not. The working languages of criticism remain now no less than previously the meta-languages which define what writing is, including what a poetry and its poetics are. The difference is that these new critical languages are saying much more than that the poem is no longer the central object of critical attention or that the film, popular culture, the CD ROM, music, the historical document, the quotation have taken its place. For the dislodgement of the poem is not separable from a pervasive shift in thinking about not just the poem per se but about the core status of activities such as "writing" and "literature." The new theories now turn attention to the world of the interface, to interactivity and to multimedia trajectories between image and mind. The sort of textual "objects" which are the object of study are no longer the imaginative and, so to speak, hand-crafted texts of poets. The practical task of writing an artefact like a poem seems to be frozen in time, locked conceptually into the notion of *métier* in the sense that Eliot, for instance, meant it when he talked about poets as "practitioners" of their art.

Things have changed considerably since that time. Writing, we are now told, must be treated as a permanently problematic instance of a much larger issue in philosophy and thought, which is to say, the issue of representation, of how texts represent the world, of how they represent differences of view and viewpoint and how they mask opposition and contradiction. In philosophical terms writing (it would seem) can never free itself from its status as a provisional moment in a theoretical schema where writing is a "philosopheme" à la Derrida. No longer a finished poem or story, a piece of writing is just one molecule in a structuring of appearance, tentative meaning and unconscious drive. This new modelling of the notion "writing" is so super-relativistic, so anxious to treat writing as a form of ongoing and never terminated textuality, that all writing gets treated as an after-effect, a supplement. The authenticity of what the writing says, even the fact that the text has an author, are similarly treated as mere facets of textuality. Writing just goes on, and never finishes or defines itself as a brilliant object. It is simply text, a text which has lost any meaningful relationship with the practice of the well-formed and definitive phrase. In such a climate of critical thought it is not too surprising that nowadays finishing on a *bon mot* raises suspicions, not a laugh.

Of course this account deliberately exaggerates the intensely theoretical cast of mind which much recent debate about literature assumes. Yet what this account brings out is the extent to which creative practice is no longer recognised as the core dimension of how we think about writing. That place is increasingly taken by philosophical discussion to do with language and text. Every creative writer writes these days with at least some level of awareness of this shift in critical consciousness. This awareness can even become an anxiety that his or her work does not identify the kind of work which critics, and by extension informed readers, see as exemplary of the latest ideas, the latest thinking, the latest media. But this very same question to do with the location of new writing in the world of contemporary ideas, of other contemporary art and media, immediately brings us back to the contextual worldly zone of the Tenth Muse. Her sphere of operations pertains directly to the placement and reception of the poet and poetry. As with all the activities of the Tenth Muse, many of the factors involved (critical reception, publishing success, acknowledgement) are largely beyond the creative artist's control.

Is it possible, for example, to *ignore* this major critical shift in the contemporary idea of writing which has occurred over the last twenty years or so? If so, the the Tenth Muse may well condemn your work to be seen as reactionary or archaic, unable to release itself from sentimentalised, already known styles of feeling. But whatever course of action the writer takes, the lack of responsive, philosophically based critical writing sets up a challenge as to how and where the work of the contemporary poet can be received. It is not so much the case that the Tenth Muse no longer engages with the poet. It is rather that in the Muse's everyday terms, critics mostly no longer care to respond with the repertoire of instruments which in earlier decades benefited poetry: close-up analysis, speculative theories to do with poetry, a honing of methods of reading, an obsession with the key figures and rhetorical devices of poetic language. All too obvious when you look through publishers' catalogues, contemporary criticism has moved its field of attention. Among the grand, highly detailed entries for popular culture, media, sociology of art, post-Lacanian criticism, hybridity, tele-theory and the like, the poet's work often appears not only as very small fry indeed but also as mere after-effect, mere symptom, of a larger cultural identity question.

The oddity is that this recent moment of media-aware, post-structuralist criticism is a moment pre-occupied to an almost unprecedented degree with issues which (formerly) were firmly embedded in the canon of poetics and the philosophy of language. Has there indeed been a period which, consciously or unconsciously, has agonised over the philosophical grounding of poetics as much as ours? For a few years indeed it seemed as if it was impossible to open a new book or read an essay without the dizzying array of terms to do with representation, identity, subjectivity, sign-values, rhetoric and so on assaulting the mind. This latterday, highly self conscious poetics is what a couple of generations of readers since the early 70s conglomerated under the numbing title "Theory." For the contemporary poet the problem has been that there is no follow-on from these theoretical obsessions. It has appeared that no matter how intense the level of concern to define and theorise notions of "represent-ation" and "writing" or to write about psyche and sign, nothing obliges anyone to pay attention to poems. A conceptual space between poems and poetics, previously peopled by literary critics, essayists and reflective readers alike, has been cleared of inhabitants. This is not so much a no man's land fought over by warring parties as a territory rigorously fenced off by the reader unfriendly philosophical nature of much recent theoretical criticism. One result is that the creative space between poetry and critical theory has disappeared, and with it the instruments by which the ideas of poetic work, of custom, of inheritance, of voice, self and psyche can be defined expertly and powerfully.

There is no doubt that the critical themes of recent critical writing are intelligent, complex and philosophically interesting – so much so that they can even fire the imagination. Once written into university courses, no bright student, no high-flyer, can avoid their influence. It is hardly surprising if "new" writers are now appearing (often award winning and freshly published) who have no trouble in reciting these epochal critical doctrines. What is more disturbing is that these doctrines' super-relativism can quickly become a mask for a pluralist yet frighteningly self assertive indifference to the qualities of the work. The poem and poetry writing seem to have been evaporating within the turn of the millennium's critical furnace. The gesture, the shell, the often absurdly exaggerated tone of "the poetic" abound. There is little of substance. Poetry is like a ghost darting about in a burning house.

3

True, there is no idyllic, permanently unchanging relationship between poet and critic. That relationship has to be constructed, as was the case in the past where the connection was for the most part carefully motivated and sustained. It is wishful thinking to believe, for instance, that the seemingly self evident verities of tonality, feeling, craft, life experience and vision, created in part as a working critical vocabulary in the period of high modernism, lacked carefully and purposefully delineated links with older, humanist styles of criticism. The view which represents the writer as a deeply experiencing and deeply experienced practitioner is itself a critical construct and not just a characterisation of a life lived fully. Similarly, practices of "creative writing," widely established in many American universities by the 1920s and 30s, did not and still do not lack a critical relationship with the then contemporary forms of humanist (theoretical and practical) criticism.

On the other side of the divide between creative practice and critical discussion, it is equally wrong to conceive past writers as philosophical *naifs* who could not hold a candle to critical debate. The writers who are now at the turn of the 21st century identified as the ancestral models of contemporary creative practice engaged productively and argumentatively with the criticism and philosophy of their times. They were not dumbfounded by, or passive victims of, critical aporia. D.H. Lawrence, whose range of friendships distantly and indirectly impacted on my own life, reacted both with and against what we would nowadays term the advanced cultural theory of his period, namely, its own version of critical truth and social identity. Similarly many of the poets of that same period (Pound, Eliot, Jarrell, Hulme, Yeats to mention a few) were so engaged with the *abîme* of the criticism co-terminous with their own work, that they wrote pages and pages of critical essays and even (sometimes complex) poetic "theory". A glance at Pound's letters or essays is sufficient to remind one of what fervour and engagement look like when a poet gets critical. These writers felt that they had not just a part, but a major role, in the criticism of their day.

The paradox, the sheer oddity, of the relation between poetry and criticism in our time is intense. The contemporary critic's work looks so confident, so well referenced, so sophisticated in relation to the major philosophical questions of its time; the poet's looks home made, handcrafted, often small and mute. Yet so many of the critical or philosophical themes sketched in a resumé of post-structuralism's key themes are part of a poetics. As such these ideas respond not just to an abstract idea of writing, or to the workings of a purely intellectual notion of conscious or sub-conscious *écriture:* they are to do with writing, with composing language in written form, with mark-making. When anyone scribbles in a notebook or logs in to a personal computer these issues surrounding writing become part of a day-to-day practice; they form the substructure of the practical matter of writing poems even if the connectedness of poems and poetics, when mapped at a more abstract level, seems to dictate an abysmally wide difference of register between the critic's pre-occupations and the poet's practices.

In fact, the cross-referencing between the two is omni-directional: the inflection of poem by poetics, and vice versa, is an inescapability. Thus, where the question of authorship and text is concerned, every poet knows the difference between the truth of "self" and the truth of the poem. Every poem – not just poems written under the auspices of the supplement – is, in this philosophical sense, a symptom of an un-conscious writing. Similarly no poet is unaware that the creative process immediately requires that you understand the differences between completeness and incompleteness in the resolution of poetic expression. For every poem is that molecule, provisionally positioned within a larger and unachievable language whether that language is that of the nation or the private mythological language of the self or the wider range of unspoken lexical meanings which every utterance entails. The modern critic, more excited by various late-modernist forms of relativistic explanation borrowed from scientific models than by poems, has preferred to deal with effects, with mass products, with items delivered by media and other electronic information systems. Poetry has largely remained the unknown (sometimes suppressed) limit case for this model of analysis.

Then there is the matter of the deferred or provisional nature of meaning which the theorist proposes. Yet every poem reckons with the question of inauthenticity and displacement in its own utterance and writing. When considered as part of the psychological issue of poetic invention, half the problem of composing poetry is to do with the poet's on-the-pulse sense of the inadequacy of spoken or written language as a vehicle for experience. After all, a poet's main critical question is rarely the "Is it good?" question of the judgmental reader. The poet's question is usually some form of: How do I get the words to do something they do not normally do? How to get language to see, to hear, to taste and touch? Does the poem say enough? Do you see the world differently when you read it? Do you know what seeing the world actually is? How to get the finished poem to be a kind of tactical leap between sense and meaning? Valéry brilliantly identified this core moment of displacement at the heart of poetic composition as a prolonged "hesitation" between sound and sense. The making of poetry asks for an engagement with these questions. You could not write unless these questions, none of which takes language and experience literally or literalistically, were the kernel of the practice.

Teaching poetry never answers the dictates of the theoretically minded critic: the poetry class will always seem too pragmatic, too willing to break out of rigorous thought when it suits. Nor will it satisfy those who are convinced that it is only some intangible x-factor, some force of will or element of self disposition which ultimately have the key role in determining the success or failure of the work. To them, teaching poetry converts it into a mere creative discourse and degrades the humanist relationship between originality of feeling and the discovery of a *métier*. To both the theorist and the sceptic, however, it must be rejoined that however out-of-kilter and confusing the moment in which poetry, the practice of being a poet and the context of critical reception find themselves, this is how the Tenth Muse prefers the world: wayward, diverse, full of opportunity. She is the Muse who controls the terms on which poems are received in their own time. She even has a stake, though not a controlling influence, in some of those circuitous pathways by which a direct knowledge of the tradition is handed on. To reduce poetry and its teaching to a textual matter or an issue primarily to do with reception and reading is to trespass on that world-sense or worldly sense indispensable in the formation of a poet. It is to fail to understand the workings of the Tenth Muse. Her world (even in post- and post-post-structuralist days) will always be individual, and fruitfully mythological: her way will still have its hidden, surrogate pathways.

For this is where poetry and the idea of teaching poetry are inescapably positioned, between the practice of a craft and inherited knowledge, between creative imagining and philosophical thinking. It can readily be conceded that no poet who teaches, no teacher who is a poet, could ever so misunderstand teaching as to be confident of its outcome. Similarly, the gap between poem, writing, textuality and theory is not stable. Critical disenchantment and writerly scepticism are constantly contradicted by new examples of interlinkage. How, for instance, does a poet respond to the latest theories about digital aesthetics, interactivity and the new interfaces? These new theories often sidestep (or perhaps just overlook) the philosophical anxiety of the post-structuralist moment. Already in other words, the philosophical context is changing. Conductivity, metaphor, association, illogical voices combining separate levels of experience, writing with imaginary spaces, these look as if they are about to become the new words of the new millennium. But these things are nothing new to poetry. If such practices become the new Glass Bead Game which the next few decades of critics, philosophers and designers will refine as a model for an emerging phase of creative thought, then poets could even look forward to it. Who knows, their *métier* might even find new allies.

land and theory [9]

*The modern individual is, above all else,
a mobile human being.*[10]

In writing about two poems, A.D. Hope's "Australia" and Les Murray's "At Min-Min Camp", my concerns are about the how – the manner and the nuance – of seeing and not directly about the thing seen. They could in this regard be termed adverbial, for they are about a qualificatory trace in all action, a trace which is also a gap between the experience of an action and its narrative. This adverbial trace (this "how") is what links these poems historically and psychologically while allowing a reading which sidesteps more classical considerations of a purely literary sort: issues such as literary origins, genre, the writer's visionary claims and the work's symbolic structure. What interests me is not straightforwardly literary but rather is a set of implicit sensory themes about location and ultimately about an aspect of poetry which (extending the idea of the "how" of seeing to include a variety of regimes of perception) I will short hand as modality. How, in other words, does the poet "go about in the world" in this or that poem? What styles of seeing and feeling occur? Which atmospheres, which climates, which assumptions about the place and texture of experience are let into the poem and which are not?

In short, such a reading momentarily fixes on adverbial aspects of place and sight and on the modality or "manner of doing" implicit in the poem. But what is also interesting is how consistent these modal figures are in each poem, almost as if a controlling mode operates deeply in the structuring of poetic experience and distributes tonalities and rhythms of perception across the poem's language. I want to suggest that there are three such figures: that of "turning around" and secondly an archaeological figure of "above/below," of layers and sediments. Typically, too, both poems make prominent a third figure, a figure of movement and journeying in relation to a grounding concept of national territory. It is a figure of mobility which relates many such Australian poems to a continuing tradition within a contemporary, more post-modern kind of vision to do with seeing and reflecting on that seeing.

Australia

"Australia" reads as a consummate achievement of a curiously an-aesthetic type of poetry which might seem to have little to do with modality.[11] It is a poem of voice and

9 First published in *Southerly* 57/2,Winter,The English Association, Sydney 1997

10 Richard Sennett, *Flesh and Stone: The Body and the City in Western Civilisation*, Faber and Faber, London, 1994, p 255

11 The full text of "Australia" is reprinted in ed. David Brooks, *A.D.Hope: Selected Poetry and Prose*, Halstead Classics, Sydney, 2000, p 54

opinion. Its sensibility and its performance of style and tone operate between common thought and significant literary form. As an ideological construction, it maps a territory held in common by expatriate visions of the local sense of things, no less than by patriotic and possibly nationalist ones. Fifty years later the story it tells of "here" and "there," of ironic displacement and of glad return (I am thinking of the famous line "there are some like me turn gladly home") still links in with the larger, latterday narrative in which a cultivated sense of permanent exile is in conflict with a rhetorical adoption of demotic "Australia" as home. Perhaps not surprisingly, "Australia" is still a major site of a mythology whose contradictions it both promotes and resolves. Strikingly, the names it offers of nation, culture, civilisation and migratory return have recently re-appeared in the guise of post-modern and post-colonial criticism.

Paradoxically, however, the poem also seems quite dated, quite out of touch with modern preoccupations. Besides, it is so famous that to read it is inevitably also to read the history of its reception. In this way, the Australia which the poem depicts is all too firmly ensconced, as textual instance, within the repertoires of "school anthology" and "nation." It is too much part of the doxa of nationalist rhetoric. For Hope this was a nation "without songs, architecture, history" whose only rescuable reference to post-modern senses of flow and trajectory is a remark about settlement as a river of immense stupidity. "Australia" clearly infringes Whitlamite, Keatingesque, left wing notions of nationalist emergence with its depressing, downgrading version of national life. "Australia" is also devastatingly ignorant of anything other than a whitefella, civilising view of settler-culture. If Hope's phrase "She is the last of lands" inevitably suggests distance from London, then similarly Hope's sense of emptiness ("She is the last of lands, the emptiest") reads now as censoring any trace of accurate settler history and any acknowledgement of Aboriginal presence. The poem's demography is inert in regard of multilingualism or multicultural forms of migration, including those of the poem's own decade.

Of course, my procedure in sketching such a reading is, no less than Hope's poem, ironic. A device to break through its *fama:* its ring of fire. For it is obvious that "Australia" is a remarkable achievement of political prophecy and stylistic control. Transferred to our doubtful post-modern days it is still current, still negative/positive and resistant. Hope's generalising, pure, aloof manner remains mesmeric.

So to understand it further, it might be necessary to pick out some terms already introduced, in particular, *myth* and *significant form.* This poem is, for example, as concerned with cultural metaphor and myth as it is transparently neo-classical in its attunement of common thought to precisely executed literary genre. Particularly, however, in its construction of implicit cultural senses of place, it becomes noticeable how a series of terms to do with assumed orders of perception and assumed and relatively unselfconscious ideas about embodiment and perspective play across "Australia". Indeed this mode of seeing is a form of over-seeing, untroubled and surveying, leaping from point of interest to point of interest and uninterested in filling in the gaps.

Modality and figure intertwine in the poem in a complex and half hidden way. The poet "sees" his geographical territory in a manner which I would term interstitial and curiously placeless, even if the out-of-the-air, overseeing mode of "Australia" is, paradoxically, the ground for the final and very famous moment of glad return.

Australia is to be read as a map or an overlay, whose points of interest are already loaded with intellectual standpoints. Strategically adopting the position (and indeed the tone: those annoying "monotonous tribes") of the colonial planner, the viewer recites the famous trans-continental distance as if from an Imperial Almanac, while indicating the coastal cities like a child tracing his finger along the pink-shaded coastal fringe. Or another example: a similar overseeing manner, moving from point to point and flattening out differences on the way, occurs in the curious river image already referred to:

> Her rivers of water drown among inland sands,
> The river of her immense stupidity
>
> Floods her monotonous tribes from Cairns to Perth...

A stupefying flood smoothes out all differences and topographical discrepancies in a journey of several thousand kilometres. This flood erases the ferment of writing, art, political opinion, economic hardship, technological change and racial difference which characterised Australia back then as they do now. Clearly, there is an implicit modal structuring at work here by which only a particular sort of terrain for an Australia can be brought into being.

At first sight of course, it might appear that the mythemes of "culture" are what carry the poem's modal structure. And it is true that a series of cultural displacements has to be brought into play here for "Australia's" thematic content to proceed. Thus, a set of oppositions build up a necessary figure of oscillation, irresolution and hesitancy; in other words, they build up the necessary conditions (much like someone stopping in the street, remembering something and turning back) by which a new order of decisiveness can be produced from the antonyms of here/there, civilisation/chatter, savagery/spirit, jungle/desert, modern thought/learned doubt, monotony/colour and so on. These oppositions, however, do not line up across a consistent cultural divide of back here/over there, no matter how much at first glance it might appear so. It is tempting for example to read "Australia" as if it performs a typically Australian moment of anti-modernism. But it does not do so, in the same way that it cannot be reduced to a poem of simple oppositions between Urbanity and Nature. Instead, the name of the country, Australia, becomes a shifter between two appositionally defined segments in the same myth of culture. According to one part of the myth, modern culture is civilising and desirable. According to another part of the myth the very same modern culture is going decadent and feral and must be avoided at all costs. This double messaging vision of Australia's place in the wider world culture operates under the sway of what looks curiously like a Kleinian good breast/bad breast sense of relationship with the other, but this in itself is still not a sufficient explanation for the poet's celebrated invoking of a moment of glad return:

> Yet there are some like me turn gladly home
> From the lush jungle of modern thought...

What must be remembered is that the creation of opposites is also the creation of a structure. The poet's hesitancy, a psychological figure constructed from opposites and from his distant overseeing manner, prepares the ground on which the acquisition of place can be "sited". But at the heart of the figure of turning there is a problem which is not just to do with cultural geography and myth. The poet introduces a.

different order of boundary and movement into his overviewing of cultural opposites. The discourse of here and over there is overtaken by another surreptitiously organised set of co-ordinates. This doubling of the theme of place is easy to overlook in "Australia's" placeless, discursive construction. For, in fact, the poem rhetorically builds two *quite distinct* "places". Between them there occurs a dramatic shift – I would say a complete fracture – at the heart of the poem's modal construction.

Put bluntly, do the last eight lines of "Australia" have anything to do with what precedes them? Many readers make the assumption that there is a logical progression here between the negative/positive view of Australia and the moment of glad return. But when read carefully it is quite clear that what the poet gladly turns back to is not his negative Australia. Nor is he literally turning away from the implied opposite of that drab nation, some colourful, intelligent Europe, for instance. What he turns from is completely unprepared for in the poem's smoothing, overseeing, mapping vision of the land, and is dropped in with surprising and carefully calculated inappropriateness. He turns from the "lush *jungle* of modern thought." The surprise is not only that this "jungle" is a placeless and largely undefined realm. It also leaps out because the word is chosen more for its metaphoric and symbolic power rather than for any literal reference to northern Queensland, say, or for that matter to Kipling. Some

> ...like me turn gladly home
> From the lush jungle of modern thought, to find
> The Arabian desert of the human mind...

Nothing has anticipated this purely intellectual move. When set against the *Arabian* – not Australian – desert of the mind which the poet now turns towards, the transcendent nature of the turn becomes fully apparent. The underlying antinomy is not between here and there, culture and savagery but between thought and mind, between wet and dry, the lush and the arid. These oppositions are fully modal, entirely to do with contrary sorts of mind-space. That earlier part of the poem, the moment of cartographic, embodied hesitation, is a prelude to a classical in-the-mind manoeuvre between thought ("modern thought") and a style of meditation. It is a choice between wet body (jungle) and dry space (Arabia), a choice made in order to glimpse some spirit which can (in Hope's words) "escape".

at min-min camp

Some fifty years later we are camping in the ruins. A.D.Hope's map is now a temporary stop-over on a journey heading inland towards the real, not the Arabian, desert. In Les Murray's "At Min-Min Camp" there is an exquisitely evoked sense of place; but it is a place in which the idyllic vision of Australia terminates. This endpoint is captured in the baroque image of a verandah which has lost its house: it is all that is left of an old station's farmhouse where Murray makes camp one night under the onset of a truly cosmological night. The night is the kind of dizzying night you can see almost every night far west on the other side of the Dividing Range. Most likely we are in the Channel country of south west Queensland, famous for its peculiar refractions of light at night, the so called "min min" effect of dancing lights.

In symbolic terms, the poet and his unnamed friends are on the way, on a journey moving through the poor but theatrically well-lit space where ordinary battlers travel "to the modern world". The moment of "seeing" is literal: irony here gives way to icon. The moment of seeing is now carried figuratively in the effect of turbid sky and lightning striking the earth along the skyline. This ruined theatre is a shelter after a dusk heat-storm of thunder and lightning:

> In the afternoon a blue storm walloped and split
> like a loose mainsail behind us. Then another
> far out on the plain fumed its corrugated walls.

> A heavy dough of cloud kept rising, and reached us.
> The speeding turbid sky went out of focus, fracturing
> continually, and poured. We made camp on a verandah

> that had lost its house. I remembered it: pitsawn pine
> lined with newspaper. People lived on treacle and rabbit
> by firelight, and slept on grain-bag quilts there.[12]

Reckoning with the inland's dramatic, beautiful weather-effects, accepting its stark history of poverty and social change, is no longer a monotonous, stupid, second-hand (Hope) kind of thing to think and talk about. They are exactly the sorts of issues which Australians (who have got more familiar with the interior now that it is no longer active hinterland but drought-struck, flood-prone, post-industrial, half-abandoned farmland) address every day. We have no doubt about the capacity of the landscape to realise concretely the spirit of Hope's savage and scarlet ("Such savage and scarlet as no green hills dare"), and perhaps no-one any longer lives timidly but somewhat thankfully on the shore.

On the other hand, we still have problems with chatter (Hope). It is only the rain which in Murray's evocative phrase dies away to conversation, to talk, to functional interchange and which ultimately leads on to a vision which is at once intimate and mythic, emotional and abstractly planetary:

> ...when the rain died away to conversation, and parted
> on refreshed increasing star-charts, there arose

> an unlikely bushfire in the ranges. The moon leaped from it,
> slim, trim, in perfect roundness. Spiderwebs palely yellow
> by firelight changed sides, and were steel-thread, diamante.

> Orange gold itself, everything the moon gave, everywhere
> was nickel silver, or that lake-submerged no-colour
> native to dreams. Sparse human lights on earth

> were solar-coloured, though: ingots of a homestead,
> amoebae that moved and twinned on distant roads...[13]

Clearly, a topographical sense is strongly felt; things and events are carefully oriented in relation to each other. But this time the architecture of the poem is to do with fragments and systems: the fragments of the verandah and the fragmented sense of a journey, the networks of overhead constellations, car lights criss-crossing on a highway, the pinpointing of distant house lights, the flickering of moon glow and striation of bush fire. "At Min-Min Camp" is a poem of darkness and networked, moving lights; it is a poem, too, where the relationship between inner dream-like

---

12 Les Murray, *Collected Poems 1961–2002*, Duffy and Snellgrove, Sydney, 2002, p 258
13 Les Murray, ibid.

senses and outer perceptions becomes tentative. The incandescence of the moon, for example, is for Murray like the semi-colour of dreamscapes.

Distinct from Hope's cartographic eye in "Australia" the mode of seeing is not predicated on the figure of the turn; it is not a seeing conditioned by hesitation and mythic contradictions. Rather (and no doubt related to that sense of greater transitiveness between inner and outer awareness) to "see" is a subliminal form of looking upwards to the approaching electric storm and, then, to the cooler and more immense night sky; while, by the same token, the viewer can also look downwards into the fissures of the earth. The body-figure, the position at the centre of the poem's modal construction, is a seeing which sees the "overhead" and the "below." Ultimately perhaps this body-figure is that of the child looking up into the face of the parent. But having looked up, the viewer will inevitably also compare that vision with the looking which fixes on the ground.

To Murray, those who, a couple of generations ago, left the half-destroyed house on the plain (what he calls "the last house") can be identified with all of humanity:

> ...You can't catch up with them now
> though it isn't long ago: when we came from the Rift Valley
> we all lived in a small star on the ground.

From this rift or hollow Murray traces an abstract origin, a broader, more archaeological sense of ancestry. It does not matter that this ancestry is not specifically Australian. Instead the overlay-style map of Hope's poem lies literally and imagistically in what Murray's poem positions as a darkness underground: that is to say, a point of origin is not located in a city "over there" but in an abstract, intellectual place in the anthropological and ethnographic record. The map of the five cities is replaced by a map of chthonic emergence and starry pin pricks. The poem's modal form is to trace the various emanations of the light in relation to this hidden ground. Thus, Aboriginal predecessors at Min-Min are "boys" who have gone off to be "wandering lights" on the plain. Humanity's ancestors are primitive men creeping towards a fire; they are "shifting faces" called to the "light's edge". Similarly the main protagonists in the poem ("we") are stranded travellers who, after being drenched by thunderbolts and then showered by starlight, huddle around the camp fire's flickering flames:

> We were drinking tea round a sheet-iron fire on the boards
> bearing chill on our shoulders, like the boys who'd slept
> on that verandah, and gone to be wandering lights
>
> lifelong on the plains...[14]

Yet none of this account does justice to this peculiarly beautiful poem's modal complexity – in particular the way in which "At Min-Min Camp" foregrounds the elements of temporal phase within the journey. This is a temporary stop-over, a stop-over freighted with time. Dwelling, it is suggested, is a temporary camp site: a moment in which a star-map of the true community is found to be fragmentary, possibly divergent. The poem is sensitive to a non-European feel for country, a feel incipiently found in styles of nomadic interlinkage. Yet no less insistently there is, as in "Australia", a point of modal fracture in the poem. Driven by the topography's overriding sublimatory demand, there is movement in the gaze, an interruptive

---

14 Les Murray, ibid.

moment in the mind, which has not been prepared for. Despite all the senses of journey, of ancestral dispersal and architectural network, a "new thing" (Murray's phrase) has to be introduced, which suddenly ties together and centralises the poet's vision.

This new thing is the sudden arrival of that most European of icons, the face. For Murray to speak of land requires that the vision of it conforms to a Christian face ("holiness, a true face, constant in all lights") whose Graeco-Byzantine fullness is at odds with the yarn-telling, story-forming lineaments of a ground-painting or an interlinkage of sacred sites, or a 4-wheel drive across the plains. To take non-European notions literally, to take them nomadically is, as the poem says, to re-invent fairy tales: it is to turn the sacred into a fairy-tale:

> Then the sacred turned fairy-tale, as always. And the new thing,
> holiness, a true face, constant in all lights,
> was still very scattered. It saved some. It is still scattered.[15]

Modally, what is still not clear is how this face (of salvation) is to be seen. Is it seen from above, like the shattered fragments of a lake system in dry country? Or do we look up and into it as if into the prismatic shatter of light through rain clouds or tree branches? However displaced, "At Min-Min Camp's" modal base remains this key signifier of contemplative human presence: the responsive face. It corresponds to a prayer image which gathers together (in an Augustinian way) the congregated city of overt and true appearances. By the end of the poem, the inference is that Australia should become a version of the City of God.

Baroque, full of leakages, thoroughly theatrical, "At Min-Min Camp" turns out to be no less a political vehicle than Hope's "Australia". Yet it is much more theological. The relations of body, self and land are those of the autonomous Christian individual and of the thinker in search of the ideal community of faith. Even if you can travel further west, you take the hope of finding this face with you. Even if you can cross the limit of European topography, you take the impulse towards communal belief with you. If the final almost self-mocking moments of the poem portray the poet in a kind of Mad Max scenery heading over ruined squatter country on the back of a stripped down truck, we are nonetheless taking with us the House of the Holy Ghost.

post-modern fragments

Les Murray has never written the poem of the next camp fire further west.

In hindsight, we know that the journey further West has been so far the achievement of the aerial, archaeological viewpoint of white and Aboriginal painters of the post-60s period – especially painters like Rover Thomas, the Papunya artists, and Olsen, Juniper, Fairweather, Wolseley and Tuckson, or photographers like Richard Wollendorp. Few poets have signalled similar preoccupations in their work, the key exception being Jennifer Rankin; but her early death prematurely ended the development of a major poetry which could interlink the themes of non-European geography, metaphoric orders of flying, a mix of lying-in-and-on-the-ground images and an inward-facing, psychological sense of movement. Some of David Campbell's final poems similarly suggest a relativistic, sedimented, mythological account of place – in particular "Menindee," "The Wimmera," "Wind in Casuarinas" or "The Niagara Café". As with

---

15 Les Murray, ibid.

the painters, whenever the poets have explored this area of the senses, it has usually been (quite literally) in the inland. Perhaps responding to the flatness of most of inland Australia, the predominant modal figure has been that of sedimentary levels, of above and below. Similarly many of the poems assume a particularly self reflexive sense of experience, a kind of gap between the artifice of the poem and the immensity of the spatial dimensions of topographical experience (both in and out of the mind.) Paradoxical though it may sound, the success of such work is that the poems deeply disguise the provisional and fractured nature of their structures in the way that Hope's and Murray's poems also strive to do.

In the main, however, it has not been in poetry where this sedimentary, mythological mode has been most explored. It has been in criticism and critical theory. Immediately when thinking of the new perceptions and new dimensions currently given to the notion of interior or the centre in Australia, the references have to be to essayists and critics like Eric Rolls, Stephen Muecke or Ross Gibson or of the work of literary geographers like George Seddon or art critic-and historian, Martin Thomas.[16] Criticism in the visual arts, together with writing about cinema and photography, have also been a primary source for a body of work which often combines memoir, history and discontinuous theoretical narratives.

Film making and painting play a part in Stephen Muecke's *No Road (Bitumen All the Way)*, an often comic compilation of post-modern traveller's tales. To take one example, visual and theoretical references abound in the way the narrator defines a potentially calamitous aesthetic difference of outlook between himself and his travelling companions, a Fred Williams influenced Moroccan painter and his wife:

> I have a Postmodernism which would like to see images of motels
> sketched against...other landscapes, layered, no real Nature, only
> palimpsests and impositions. Thus, the extensions to the Halls Creek Hotel,
> a short flight to the Bungles, are perfect Dallas – Southfork ranchero
> style – added to the old colonial pub, and with elements ofthe glass
> postmodern arch thrown in. We are camped beside the hotel, red dust
> getting into everything, the tent, the car, we tramp it into the hotel then
> into the front bar to play pool. Red suffuses the sky at sunset, and there
> would be a red wash in this painting I am imagining...[17]

In some cases writing about the modal experience of the inland has been directly the work of artists as is the case of painter and installation artist Kim Mahood's *Craft for a Dry Lake*, an account of an artist's return to her childhood home in the Tanami Desert. Often for her, the identification with land is literal, physical and performative not least in her sense of the connection between personal beauty and environment. An intense sense of return and reflexiveness is captured in what she calls the "curious experience" of growing up "in mythological country":

---

16 Among these writings, I would include Eric Rolls's *A Million Wild Acres* (Penguin, Melbourne 1984), Krim Benterrak, Stephen Muecke and Paddy Roe's *Reading the Country: Introduction to Nomadology* (Fremantle Arts Centre Press, Fremantle,1984), George Seddon's *Landprints: Reflections on Place and Landscape* (Cambridge University Press, Cambridge, 1997) and Ross Gibson's *South of the West: Post-colonialism and the Narrative Construction of Australia* (Indiana University Press, Bloomington 1992.) Martin Thomas's study of European and Aboriginal perceptions of the Blue Mountains, *The Artificial Horizon*, appeared in 2003.
17 Stephen Muecke, *No Road (Bitumen All the Way)*, Fremantle Arts Centre Press, Fremantle, 1997, p 29

It is possibly like being very beautiful. It is the thing people notice about you, that makes you different and unique. It becomes the way you identify yourself. This is where I come from. This is my country. This is me. [18]

Relativism of position – a sense of physical movement and a recursive psychological movement (in this case, between levels seen from above) – is what fascinates in an account given by the art critic, Noel Sheridan, when he writes of going for a walk at the Warburton community in central Western Australia. It is as as if he is already experiencing something of the camp west of Min-Min:

Gary Proctor arranged that we could travel great distances in the Toyota with a group of elderly Aboriginal people to see certain important places and rock carvings in the Warburton area. The sense of the relativity of distance within this journey was something which could not be brought to Perth. After a while it seemed to me that there was no middle ground to the experience of the landscape; things were either very far away or microscopically close. Tommy Simms, our guide, might draw our attention to a formation on the horizon and immediately relate it to some small stones at our feet. The transition for him, and the other Aboriginal people in the group seemed effortless but I could almost feel my eyes clicking into focus trying to follow the trajectory his hand indicated. Scale too was disordered: some huge rock might be detail in an account that had as its source some cluster of tiny pebbles; the footprint of an animal was often bigger than the animal.[19]

It is wonderful. And one admires Sheridan's frank, awkwardly intellectual admission that "it was the anchor of an epistemology of modernist perception which first caught and then engaged me with Aboriginal art". It was, in short, modernist art-theory and the problematics of the flat picture-plane which took him off to Warburton. Looked at closely, however, this is also a writing which constructs a series of micro-turns, both rhetorically and literally. These turns occur not once as in "Australia" but repeatedly, between pebble and horizon, between Warburton and Perth, between the far and the close, between the big and the little, between white and black. The eye is constantly turning back. The construction of "seeing" is that of hidden cinematic reverse shots. And at the same time there is the sense of an account of an experience which leaves it just there, as just that: an intelligent experience whose telling comes perilously close to repeating all the clichés of the explorer with his native guide. And which both fails, and honestly refuses, to escape from that ironic placement.

Could there indeed be any modally free position from which to reflect on that experience? Poetry, of course, almost inevitably foregrounds the embodied lived sense of experience, but theory and reflection too cannot escape from modal conditions similar to those with which the poet works. No less than poems, contemporary forms of post-modern and post-colonial theory, especially the kinds found around the university, carry with them constant traces of their perceptual regimes; often (and in this regard they are less interesting than poetry) they offer little more than the surface of the theorist's modal artifice. This is perhaps why so many contemporary cultural theories can be so quickly reduced to moralising or vague abstraction: erasing contradiction, unconscious of their metaphors, such theories offer redemptive and

18 Kim Mahood, *Craft for a Dry Lake*, Transworld, Sydney, 2000, p 250

19 Noel Sheridan, *Yarnangu Ngaanya: Our Land – Our Body*, Perth Institute of Contemporary Arts, Perth,1993, p 75

apocalyptic visions. Thus the terms country and land can easily lose their connection with Sheridan's "epistemology" when reduced to being merely an academic strategy within theorised accounts of reading or when invoked for nationalist political ends. Experience, momentariness, the phenomenology of the senses get lost, left behind. What results, when drained of any awareness of the modal limits of thought, is often a bizarre host of purely operational terms such as intermediacy, mimicry, trans-territorialism, spatiality, vectors and pluralisms of various guises. Theories, in other words: ideas littering an ill-defined ground. After all, the 90s were the Star Trek decade in which, year by year, we saw the invention of model after model of purely cerebral vehicles for crossing "the land".

Not all such models, it is true, deserve to be abandoned. It could be argued that the acquisition of a sense of living at a European edge *within our own* country rather than *on the edge of* an external European communication zone marks a paradigm shift at a profound cultural level. Thus, for instance, a historian such as Paul Carter, commenting on the work of Centralian anthropologist and Arrernte translator T.G.H. Strehlow, recommends a style of intermediate poetics for Australian writing, a between-two-worlds modality or a space between two mind-sets. Here too we encounter a metaphoric projection entirely dependent on the turn. Carter is looking forward in order to look back, a turn carried in the rhetorical manoeuvres (turns) of the theorist's own lively writing as much as it is carried in documentation or evidence:

> The agile warrior and the light-footed orator share a capacity to respond creatively, one might say baroquely, to historical contingencies; the well-armed goddess of eloquence is appropriately associated with them both. In the will to invent, in the gift of improvisation perhaps, lies a key to the creation of Strehlow's new Australian poetry. If so, it will be the gifts of spontaneous free association which will be privileged in the new poetry...But before running ahead like this, and in the process identifying rhetorical ingenuity with poetic inspiration, we need to be aware how much it identifies a Newtonian world-view. What for example, can it mean to talk about wilful inventiveness in a world not governed by notions of equal and opposite forces and a space that is neutral, empty?[20]

In this example, back and forth runs the glancing eye, setting up its own architecture of contrarieties and opposites in order for the theorist/see-er to be able to turn decisively and spin a new theoretical trope. Elsewhere, Carter literalises this trope, this spin-on-a-point, as a foot impressing the ground as it brings into being an indeterminate zone which Carter calls "vibrating tracks". Such prints and tracks do not lead on; they can be read backwards and forwards. The foot turns by virtue of the track's pointing in any direction. Clearly, the real turn here is sublimatory and intuitive, a move made only in the mind more or less as if Carter is trying to account for some impulse carried autonomically through the body's nervous system. We go where we go, so to speak. Somewhat problematically perhaps, what this authenticating return of savage agility and of direction free wilderness lacks is the modal feature which is crucial to Hope's poem: its fracture under the pressure of the poet's recognition (in opposition to a fluently theoretical projection) of human limit and dilemma. Carter's agility operates in some neurological, unspoken instant. The strength of Hope's poem is its ironic distancing effect, its wiliness.

---

20 Paul Carter, *The Lie of the Land,* Faber and Faber, 1996, p 319

the land, the land

Modality, that pressure of the adverbial trace, insists on a richer, more variable and more fleshed-out function than any kind of theorised seeing or over-determined notion of mobility can lend itself to. What is this function, then? Can it be named as some sort of "feeling-for-place" or a deeply acquired understanding and sensing of one's location? Insofar as this function is implicated in indeterminacy or an uncertainty in reading a land-form (as post-colonialists might wish it), then perhaps what occurs semi-spontaneously is more like what the ancients called geomancy : a sense of the magic of a place, a knowledge derived from it (by looking at its light changes, its weathers, its drynesses and thinnesses of soil, the passage of birds and animals across it, the striations and surfaces which form it) and an intuitive attraction or connectedness with its particulars (trees, stones, houses, slopes). Geomancy, it could readily be conceded, suggests a practice too ritualised and orderly for what in fact occurs when one knows a place or longs for it; for what the adverbial trace is pointing to in such seeing is a sensing of the world which is not just already interpretable and culturally meaningful but which is also beyond code. Such an awareness is that memory sense, that sense of familiarity, which has been in abeyance until the moment of return arrives. Years later long after you had forgotten the place and never imagined returning, you drive through the same deep hinterland valley plain. The flash of light on water, the pollarded willows, the riverside train tracks, the flat space before the background of magenta, eroded hills all return in an instant as if they have never been out of mind. Even micro-details like washed out road-edges, or the spacing of fence posts, float back present to the eye as if they have been held in perfect recall for decades.

Counterposed against purely theoretical vision, such experiential senses of place work against the pressure towards a spectacular telling of the nexus of language, body sense and and movement. Theory, on the other hand, inevitably reduces being to a being which is largely theoretical, that is to say, held between geometrical points, totally visibilised. So when the nexus of language, body-sense and movement is represented symbolically in a theoretical way, its human dimension will quite likely be pictured through a mode of mobility whether on the track, in space, in the truck, or pivoting on a step in a voyage as the ship (and the gaze) turns back home. This nexus (as with the turn) seems inextricably caught up with the way the eye distances itself from the thing seen and, more, treats the relationship between body and space as primarily ballistic. Such representations are highly visible, conscious and overt, tending to downplay what is hidden, covert or atmospheric. The familiar sense which returns from abeyance is simply not directed enough or smartly informative enough to satisfy theory's requirements for a modelling of experience. It does not conform to what a theorised seeing requires: it cannot be reduced to a glance shot out, or a bird or a bullet in mid-flight.

It is important in this context not to forget those other ideas and practices, no less theorised, which relate inside and outside, mind-state and land-state, topographical attributes and meditative powers. In the European tradition these other themes are mainly not to be found in architectural and painterly discourses, but in discourses not normally considered "land-based" in a straightforward sense of the term. For instance, anatomical, medical theories of the body, ancient theories of body heat and humours, no less than modern theories of blood-flow and neurological networking, of transplant and gene code modification. Similarly cultural practices around birth, rituals to do with death, sexual practices and physical culture in general all contribute to our sense of placement and embodiment. When, for example, urban historian Richard Sennett finds that "(European) civilisation from its origins has been challenged by the body in pain", then this is largely because:

> dominant images of the body have cracked apart in the process of being impressed on the city. A master image of the body inherently invites ambivalence among the people it rules, for every human body is physically idiosyncratic, and every human body feels contradictory physical desires.[21]

Sennett stresses that the placement of the body in space is never entirely open to a ballistic, anatomical, geometricised form of analysis, never totally open to the rational light and the clear-minded sky, nor clear about *its* relation to the connection between earth and sky. Similarly, the connection between discourses which analyse the body and those which represent the environment will be dialectical and evolving. A more intuitive, a less consciously visualising approach inevitably entails a response to the difficulty in building, projecting and defining a sense of "place". The Japanese environmental engineer, Tadahiko Higuchi, very usefully refers to this difficulty as a fracturing which occurs between conscious and unconscious desire by which

> (we) have ceased to be able unconsciously to develop land in such a way as to conform to nature...Retrospectively, it appears we know all too little about nature, and what we know amounts to theories which enable us to deform it.[22]

Is it perhaps this difficulty in dealing with such indeterminacy, with such unconscious factors, that leads to the resoluteness with which theories and poems strive to *complete* a "figure" of the other? The pressure is to put something stable, something overt and visible in place. This is often literally captured in, say, the figure standing in the landscape or the unforgettable detail which stands for a moment spent in a place. But equally is it not in these figures that the tell-tale trace and symptom unconsciously appear? This is why what was, first off, termed an adverbial reading reveals its further shadow-narrative: a story, certainly, but one always lurking in the shadows or hidden by the brilliance of the thing in view. It is a story which is never fully tellable, whose recitation (as it was in Les Murray's poem) is nuance and fragment. For no matter how attentive to the modal construction of place, its hesitancies and its aerial layers, a full self reflexiveness and a transparent rendition of the place-in-time (the here, the now) simply cannot happen. The gap between experience and narrative, the space of the absent adverb, remains apparent. The problem of mode and mood does not go away. In the end it is what tells us that this time, this place, are real.

---

21 Richard Sennett, op cit, p. 24

22 Tadahiko Higuchi, *The Visual and Spatial Structure of Landscapes*, trans Charles Terry, MIT, 1983, p 191

robert gray
and the revision of the senses [23]

*H*e has been described as a poet of the senses, a poet of sensory understanding and a poet whose life view is devoted to the phenomena of the natural world. He has been described also as a Buddhist, a landscapist who re-envisions the "landtalk" of coastal Australia from a Zen perspective and whose work accordingly is a major contribution to that slow shifting of continental purpose in turn of the millennium Australia, our re-thinking and re-positioning of ourselves imaginatively and politically on the edge of South East Asia. He is seen too as the Australian poet who, standing out from and often disagreeing with his peers, has both practised and publicly argued for clarity and for imagistic richness in poetry. He has been seen as the dogged opponent of reader-hostile "experimentalism" and of the empty American-influenced "internationalism" which many of his generation of Australian poets engaged in.

All of these ways of talking about Robert Gray's poetry are accurate, defining as they do three of the major characteristics of his poetry: its sensuous materialism, the often melancholy ethos of the poetry's seriousness and the poet's undoubted repugnance towards mere manner and emptily trendy gesture. These aspects of his work have largely been responsible for the establishment of a critical consensus which links Gray's poetry with the view which Gray himself quotes from Ezra Pound that "(w)ith the natural object, an artist has all he needs to express himself" ("At The Inlet").[24] It is Gray too who has drawn what is the inevitable corollary of this by now unfashionable view of poetry, that if "the intellectually chic,/with their novelties and self-regard" ("The Trendies") denigrate his poems, he is quite happy with that.[25]

This 1998 *New Selected Poems* is a chance to look again at Gray's work. Gray has always been a careful reviser and re-writer of his poetry. There was a previous *Selected* a few years back, which did what most such volumes do by way of re-circulating poems from individual volumes which have gone out of print or are no longer on the shelf. But this *New Selected Poems*, to a much greater degree shows Gray going through many of his poems almost unnoticeably changing a word here, a word there, dropping a line or a half a line. There are many such changes. They will present future editors with significant scholarly choices for, subtle and scarcely noticeable as they seem at first sight, they mark not just a pointing up or a highlighting of something the writer has later come to think unclear. These changes often mark changes of mood so significant that they are tantamount to a change of idea. There is a drift or an overall

---

23 An earlier version of this essay appeared in *Boxkite: A Journal of Poetry and Poetics 2*, The Poetics Foundation, Sydney, 1999. Sections appeared in a review of the individual volume *Lineations* in *Heat* 4, Winter 1997.

24 Robert Gray, *New Selected Poems*, Duffy and Snellgrove, Sydney, 1998, p 140. All references are to the more accurate and corrected Second Edition.

25 Robert Gray, *Lineations*, Duffy and Snellgrove, Sydney, 1996, p 83

pattern in these changes too. When their influences are totalled across the work there is the sense that they reflect a desire on Gray's part to achieve a greater humanisation of the poetry, a greater reliance on human presence and human problem. They lessen the sense that Gray is a poet of impersonal seeing, a poet for whom the visible object predominates in his sense of the world.

True, this growing sense of an increasing interest in subject-matter which can deal with a wider, more dramatic range of human perplexity and which cannot, in any one-off and neutral way, negotiate the shape of perceptions and things is not just a sudden outgrowth in the new volume. It has been developing as one of the hallmarks of later poems from the 1993 volume *Certain Things* on. But in this new selection of his work he has written this later interest in human presence and the darkness of human motive back into some of the earlier work. He seems, indeed, to have undertaken the task of revising as a task of de-aestheticisation and as an attempt at the removal of the gestural and the abstract. Gray was lavishly praised early on for the visual intensity and the optical purity of his poems. His later work, however, is just as likely to have moments of deep poignancy and self irony about that very same visual intensity. You find this ironic self deprecation in a poem like "In Thin Air" (first published in *Certain Things*) where he reflects on his youthful anxiety and uncomfortableness, his sense of estrangement from the world and on how, far from rejoicing in the visible, he felt condemned to just looking. Or as he puts it, "My life, I imagined, must be a hymn to the optic nerve." But now:

> (it) seems that I've gone far enough
> to be offered normal life...[26]

Or again, but phrased in a more generalising way:

> Existence must come of itself, and it goes on and on without a
>   reason, just because it is.
> In human consciousness, it produced an eye. It has arrived where
>   it might understand. Perhaps it cannot bear this.[27]

In other words, deeper and more complex experiences, the bluntness of that sense that "it goes on and on without a reason", have led his poetry towards psychologically more complex level of emotion. It is this more provisional and more tensely narrated sense of the world which has been written back into and across earlier poems.

Two brief examples from many. An early published (1978) version of the poem "Old House" ends with an optically brilliant eye-catching image of a white coat down a corridor – in this case the corridor of light across water of what might be Sydney Harbour or some adjacent area of the New South Wales coast. "Down the sea's vast corridor," he writes, "a white coat." Here, reflecting the manoeuvring of a yacht, are the relevant lines:

> The crack of its going-about
> and the cry
> of a gull, covering them with its wings, echoed
> in the bare verandah.
> Down the sea's vast corridor, a white coat.[28]

---

26 Robert Gray, *New Selected Poems*, op cit, p 218

27 op.cit., "A Testimony", p 220

28 Robert Gray, *Grass Script*, Angus and Robertson, Sydney, 1978, p 4

He could be looking at a triangular sail shape in a Brett Whiteley painting or at a yacht image by Tom Carment. The image of the white coat optically, and pictorially, resonates with the boat-sail. The effect is precise, imagistic, semi-abstract, no more than mildly suggestive of whomever it may be who wears a "white coat". In the later corrected version of the poem, however, this image is sharply localised and humanised as "Down an institution's corridor, a white coat:"

> The crack of its going-about,
> and the cry
> of a gull, echoed
> in the bare verandah.
> Down an institution's corridor, a white coat.[29]

Someone who does not know Sydney might be at first puzzled by the degree of precise locality now inferred by the image and its human reference to a doctor or a nurse: Gray is probably thinking of one of the old colonial houses along the Harbour foreshore which for many years was used as a mental hospital. Sure, taken as a whole the poem does not require this kind of additional geographical knowledge from a reader; the old house could be any Australian sea-side mansion converted into an institution. The point is that the abstract reference via painting has been replaced by a much more bleak, much more substantial reference to human suffering, to the pain occurring at the edge of a vista of great beauty. The viewpoint is not just that of an eye which makes aesthetic linkages for largely pictorial reasons – a reflex, that is, of the optical nerve; it is the fleshed seeing of a particular man. The beauty of the scene is narrated against the sickness or madness which the space around the viewer, up-front in the old house, contains.

The second example comes from one of Gray's many sequences of interlinked haiku style poems. Partly Japanese influenced, partly influenced by the Spanish way of writing poems as interlinked strophes or "versos" in the manner of Machado, Gray has made this form one of his own. *New Selected Poems* prints the poem "17 Poems" as a replacement for the 1978 "21 Poems". The differences are considerable, with entirely new material introduced and several earlier fragments excised. The new poem is darker, more mood driven; the implied narrative is more many-sided, achieving a more complex kind of glancing coherence. Whereas the original poem ends with a classic Australian image of a sun-filled verandah and of stifling siesta-like heat, blasting the reader with brilliant light and a suspended moment of intense perception, the new poem goes on to an extra strophe which finishes the sequence on a more melancholy and blank note:

> A long twilight,
> milky grey. Raindrops on the window,
> gulls on the grass.[30]

The bright summer day has had its change; a storm has moved in, the temperature dropped. In this new later version, Gray not only observes a different event, but signals a greater sense of instability in things and an immersion of seeing in the changing nature of events. The poem deals much more, in other words, with *how* a person, a particular person, sees. It is not just an instance of a how "a thing" (i.e. a perfect

---

29 Robert Gray, *New Selected Poems*, op cit, p 46
30 op cit, p 93

robert gray and the revision of the senses

moment, a perfect abstract object, a brilliant instant of observation) is abstractly constructed (out there, so to speak).

The tracing of these hundreds of changes will be someone's future task. The reason for mentioning that task now is to indicate the degree to which Gray is partly misrepresented when defined only as a poet of sensation or as a literal naturalist of the senses and of nature. His attentiveness is an attentiveness to things out there, but it is also an attentiveness to the workings of the poem. Poem by poem, there is an enormous care as to how a poem truthfully organises a glimpse of the world; and in this respect, he is as much what I would term a poet of the book as he is a poet of nature. Each poem provides its own framework for a provisional sense or sample of a natural occurrence which it can treat and which it realises imagistically and experientially. But there is no fixity: the poem is not text or discourse, but an expression of a trans- itive relation with things. Each poem carries in it a trace or a charge of sensation which moves between poem and reader. Language, to be sure, is the medium in which this transitiveness can occur, but it is also the medium which, if inflected with an inadequate degree of intensity and accuracy, can block up the senses, muddying them and confusing them.

The emphasis here is on a long ago established (and not a post-modern) notion of reading, reading as imaginative re-creation, reading as re-imaging of what is felt and seen. Gray's poetry denies (is opposed to) the latterday idea of reading which characterises reading as a form of further textual "writing" among a limitless play of signs. Gray's reading insists upon a meditative core at the heart of the reading process. It is hard to find a comparable poet who, writing today, so successfully re-invents this thoroughly "early" modernist notion of poetry and its interface with reading. This sense of re-creation is effectively the assertion that there is a direct connection between things and a poetic expression according to which the fulfilment of a life is, as he says, found "in the contemplation of matter".[31] This is what poems do: they allow that necessary contemplation, they benefit that fulfilment. They are *exempla* not from The Book of Nature in a scholastic sense, but from the shifting, illusory, relativistic and psychoanalytic nature of our own times. Spending time with the *New Selected Poems* is to be asked to read with a particular consciousness of how poems are reiterated meditational spaces of this sort, transacted between him and his reader. It is to acknowledge how reading the poems, no less than the writing of them, is to do with that state of mind which he at one point describes as "the best place", namely, the sense of being alone. This is the writer's and the recreational reader's paradise: "...the night before you./ The rain overwhelms itself outside. It is happiness."[32]

In the twenty or so years work selected here you follow Gray in his constant re- establishing of the terms upon which that meditational space comes into focus and, in particular, in watching what disturbs it. For as the poetry grows and matures, this question of what disturbs meditation becomes increasingly pressing, increasingly hard to avoid. It becomes more significant perhaps than the the matter of what frames perception and what constitutes the image, those matters of the early poems. This is why among the finest poems here are the difficult, anxious pieces about human

31 op cit, "At The Inlet", p 142
32 op cit, "The best place..." p 117

violence and about what Gray seems to regard as virtually a hard-wired, instinctual incapacity in human nature to deal with its "pure appetite," with what is "below / and before the mind."[33] ("The Shark") In earlier poems, Gray could play the *double entendre* of matter, that is, of thing and subject. There, punning on the illusion of a truthfulness in images, he could write, as in "A Day at Bellingen," of how the mind "*lies* once more beneath the truth of the body" (italics added):

> Now the mind is turned down, like a gas flame
> in a dark kitchen,
> where the wind and all the night sounds can again be heard.
> It lies once more beneath the truth of the body.[34]

Compared with the earlier poetry of meditational reflection on momentary illusion the later work is less interventive, more skeptical, more attentive to the necessary interplay between light and dark.

This new previously unaccounted-for quality in the later work is, in part, to do with a shift in Gray's voicing of the poems: a more assertive, directly voiced presence of the poet begins to appear. Later poems, for example, those collected in the 1996 volume *Lineations,* are much less constructed as landscapist and descriptive, and are more powerfully constructed as psychological moments, dependent on the tonal qualities of the spoken word as much as on their visual and painterly envisioning. In "Flight at Dusk," for example, the experience of flying through a storm in a small commercial plane instead of inspiring a descriptive scene or a meditation on resolved and individuated details in a visually dramatic moment offers a musically organised, single drive towards an abrupt, quirky and quite shocking conclusion. It is hard to demonstrate the workings of these new logistics in Gray's poetry without quoting long stretches of whole poems. "Flight at Dusk's" ending gives something of the "feel" of this more complex, energised talking in the poetry as the plane cruising at 18,000 feet manoeuvres round the weather and the passenger feels that sense of arbitrary fear which such events inspire:

> I turn to incomplete work
> spread on my lap. When next I look
> the moon I had seen, a fine bowl dripping
> one star, where it tilted, is vanishing,
> and the stripe of ultramarine, lit
> like an ad for a Turkish sweet.
> I feel, though I keep on working here carefully,
> disgust. So passive, so arbitrary.[35]

Read in context, the last line is withering: what it voices comes through as an affront. To whom is it addressed: to himself, when caught in a situation which renders even poetry meaningless and trivial? Or are these words addressed to the storm or to the technologically inspired set of forces which allows humans to float perilously in mid-air while storms bombard the planet?

This more urgent, more questioning sense of voicing is found everywhere in the later work. In "Nambucca Heads", for example, a tighter, more formal organisation of

---

33 op cit, "The Shark", p 185
34 op cit, "A Day at Bellingen", p 127
35 op cit, "Flight at Dusk", p 279

the verse leads to final lines which move through and beyond a purely imagistic conclusion into a climax of unrestrained lyrical outcry:

> Still this flecked ocean, blazing like
> a furnace, after a night's work,
> breathes mildness. O white Pacific.[36]

Similarly in a more recent poem such as "Version" we encounter a formality whose voice reflects a sustained undercurrent in all lyric poetry: the stillness of an inhuman and subvocal voice, that voice which is always hovering on the edge of (and under) the ear. As if responding to it, Gray writes in this poem of a pressure which is more than a characteristic of each individual's culturally formed psyche:

> All one has might as well be water dangling
> where birds light upon
> the boughs – of a sudden there has come a wing
> and it's shattered and gone.
> What we are is this pressure, that's not our own;
> unrelieved, redeployed.[37]

The new energy involved in this later work is (as the reference to a non-individual "pressure" might suggest) more than a matter of voicing. It has more to do with the way Gray is now defining experience as a momentary evolution of perception, conditioned both by the externally visible world and by a series of threshold and perhaps unconscious associations. The youthful poet of the objective image, the poet of surface, light and external landscape, is also now a poet who can carry out raids on the subconscious and liminal areas of his poetry.

Thus, a long poem like "A Garage" is worth lingering over. Superficially it is a poem which explores in minuscule detail the uncanny emotional impact of pulling up one day at a country petrol station:

> In one of the side streets
> of a small hot town
> off the highway
> I notice the garage,
> its white boards peeling
> among the grey paling fences.
> There was a lone petrol pump
> from the sixties, perhaps,
> out in the sun-blaze.

It is less a poem of the everyday event than a poem of subconscious drive and it turns out that it is the "human scale / and humanoid appearance" of the bowser which link in with Gray's thoughts. What results is mythic and ironic at the same time, a poem in which ultimately his experience is that of a

> ...blackness that was opaque
> as the diversions
> of the tunnelling heart.[38]

36 op cit, "Nambucca Heads", p 265
37 op cit, "Version", p 268
38 op cit, "A Garage", p 277

In like manner, at one point in this remarkable poem he asks from where did the petrol pump's "almost avoidable sense/ of sacrifice and remorse" arise? In other words where do these strangely associated feelings come from? How do we see and what do we see when, as he says, "our feelings/ are blown through us"?

In later poems like "Note," "Isolate Evenings," "Acceptance Speech", "Sapientia Lachrimarum" and "By a candlegrease moon..." we encounter a reckoning with the fragmentation of the poet's psyche in this underlying "opaque" void, a reckoning which marks a change of direction away from the impersonality of the image towards a stronger awareness that poems are psychologically intonated, and that they carry the marks and after-effects of subliminal experience and of half-formed, uninvestigable senses of the world. It is, I think, the assertiveness of the poet's presence in these poems and their tighter, formal organisation which allow Gray new moments of threshold insight, of unselfconscious anxiety and impressionistic richness. They are the moments of interdependence and indivisibility in everyday human experience which he defines in "Acceptance Speech", a deeply sense-oriented, at one point erotic poem about mystical awakening, as those moments "which you did not understand in all your other lives".[39]

There is, in other words, a change of emphasis, a change which would make one read the earlier work differently even if Gray had not himself patiently revised it. Sure, there is no claim here to a radical shift of the way the poet structures his poetry in the way that Helen Vendler talks about such changes as a "breaking of style" in the work of some modern poets, that is to say, an involuntary invention of a radical change in style.[40] Instead, earlier and later work can be read according to a trajectory along which the relationship between nature and human experience becomes harder to fathom, more intimate and more attuned to the negative force of the instinctual. This is a poetry in which the abstract resolution of visual experience is no longer the brilliant flash of a white sail across the ocean but more that of a later dusk landscape at Bellingen where:

> (p)ointing everywhere, the dead trees gesture
> as if they'd been in panic when they died.[41]

This longer trajectory suggests something else too. Robert Gray is a watcher and traveller. If he is a poet of the book, a poet who is constantly inclined to re-write the transitive nature of experience, then the assembled scenes which constitute the natural lessons of his poetry are starting to seem more and more like intense, fleeting glimpses of an atomised, relativistic universe of nature and human beings. There is an analogy here between Gray travelling through his Australian natural world and other poets who have travelled through their landscapes of mind and nature. This journey through shifting country is one of the ultimate figures for poetry. It was, for instance, Dante's, travelling through his own post-mortem, shape-changing country. The Dante reference to Gray is not accidental: the connection is explicitly made in key poems like "Flames and Dangling Wire" or via the *terza rima* format of the more recent "Sapientia

39 op cit, "Acceptance Speech", p 271
40 Helen Vendler, *The Breaking of Style: Hopkins, Heaney, Graham*, Harvard University Press, Cambridge, Mass., 1995, pp 1-7
41 Robert Gray, op cit, "Wintry Dusk", Bellingen, p. 293

Lachrimarum". Ultimately I think that Gray's task will turn out to have been the assemblage of a vision, more Buddhist and more secular perhaps than his antecedents', but similar in its complex and transient negotiation of the relations between truth and illusion. It is striking indeed that the originality of Gray's vision – that "optic *nerve* " – is in the final analysis of this devotional sort.

horizons of the name [42]

 *A*bout two-thirds of the way through the 1995 selected edition of Kevin Hart's poems there is a line in which he writes of:

> The nameless one, the surname of all things.[43]

This "nameless one" is given many names in the poem. It is, for example, "the darkness between two stars". It is also the darkness "between two thoughts". It is what occurs when (in Hart's phrase) "the web of names is brushed aside from things". It is most importantly what is revealed when even "the ocean's name is quietly washed away".

Yet what is left after this washing away is, as the line just quoted calmly states, both nameless and surname. It is both beyond language and yet at the same time a kind of "over"-name and proper name. Even the ocean, a key image of the unconscious and of the unfathomable depth of experience, cannot give it a name. For this "whatever" left over when the tide goes out is not some sort of exposed ocean-floor or debris of primal forms. Hart talks instead of an act or moment of revealing, a something which is (to quote his words) "an energy," a revealing of "the thing itself". It is as if he is talking about a nameless event or an unnamed moment of realisation.

"Facing the Pacific at Night" where this line about namelessness occurs is one of Hart's finest poems. The poem is about driving to see the ocean, both the real Pacific but also the ocean in the mind of a sleeping child. It captures the excitement and mystery of such experiences. By the end of the poem this sea has become the seascape which, when retrospected upon as an adult,

> quietly moves within your ear
> And flashes in your eyes

while simultaneously it is also

> ... the silent place

> Outside the world we know is here and now,
> Between two thoughts, a child that does not grow,
> A silence undressing words, a nameless love.

A rapid concatenating movement occurs in the in-between space of those "two thoughts". For the experience has become so full and so many sided that a typical

---

42 An earlier version was published in *Ulitarra* 10, 1996

43 Kevin Hart, *New and Selected Poems*, Angus and Robertson, Sydney, 1995, p 116 An expanded new Selected Edition appeared with Paper Bark Press in 2002.

childhood experience of being taken to see the sea can be re-expressed symbolically at the end of the poem as the action of a mother undressing her child.

This sort of expertly handled, nearly unnoticeable move between what is memory and what is physical embodiment is common in Hart's poems. A transaction, a kind of hidden narrative occurs almost as if the poetic experience is a demonstration of how an energised state of seeing and feeling can momentarily undergo transformation from one thing to another thing and then another thing and another thing. Thus the sea is darkness, then a childhood memory, then an energy, and then a mother figure attending to a child. But then this mother presence undergoes a further hinted mutation as if it is like a Madonna taking the infant out of his swaddling bands. The whole poem expands and deepens once this is understood. For now we can see that the image of those final lines reworks the traditional iconography of the Virgin holding the naked, infant Word (the unspeaking, pre-linguistic Christ-child) in her arms. Even this, too, is not sufficient as a way of accounting for what Hart is doing. For ending his poem the way he does, he not only re-works this image, he radically re-thinks it. For him, this revelation of the nameless and the naked returns to that underlying theme in the poem: of words, of the The Name as a matter of language. A tending, nurturing silence undresses words.

"Facing the Pacific At Night" grows from major, common and omnipresent feelings, feelings which all of us have had, experiences like going to see the sea, experiences of a sense of otherness beyond language, of a deep and inexpressible sense of how the presence of your parents continues to haunt you in adult life. This use of an interlinked resonant structure of association is very typical of Hart's imaginary world. Often locating his poems in emotional senses which are big threshold awarenesses he writes from and about feelings which everyone has had but which it is often difficult to name in a single image or to describe in a single story. They are basic yet very intimate feelings which form a common background "feel" of everyday senses of identity and which because of that intimate ordinariness are often lost to view or quickly forgotten about.

***

This attentiveness to common, familiar and yet nameless emotion is a hall mark of his best work. Reading him, there is always some such moment of entrancement and entanglement, as if he is a poet for whom nothing is ever just complex nor ever just simple. A similar moment is to be found, for instance, in "Dark Angel", a later poem. The dark angel gives a name to another prolonged childhood sense of the world, a sense of stillness and atmosphere at night when a child is falling asleep. This atmosphere is neither a place exactly nor a scene nor a sound but rather a stillness or a "sound of darkness" which

> somehow found its way into my sleep.[44]

That brief, seemingly simple line offers an inadvertent clue to how the whole poem enacts the movement of a sound entering and unconsciously lodging in the mind:

> It was our old poinsettia, straight from hell,
> Its full-moon perfume wafting through the house...
>
> Or fine mosquitoes, rising from the river
> Just coiling in the dark there, down the road...[45]

---

44 Hart op cit, p 167
45 Hart, ibid

The sound seems to require a particular kind of attentiveness, or deep listening, staying ingrained in the mind just beneath threshold awareness as if it is being heard past the edge of ordinary perception. He is describing, for example, that sort of listening which continues when the rest of the world falls away over the edge of sleep. Or it could be that constant inner listening which regularly calls us back to ourselves whether asleep or awake. Like "Facing the Pacific at Night", once the sense of threshold awareness is enacted in the poem, "Dark Angel" never fixes on a singular reference for its key term. Though it is only "a touch away" what is heard is not just his mother's voice or the sounds outside in the darkness but also the sound of a darkly sub-vocal presence.

Hart regularly operates on this border where names lose their singularity, and where transient energy states and shifts in perception occur. The latency here comes not from being vague or merely atmospheric. Indeed Hart writes with complexity and precision, as if sensitised to a limit which is totally familiar to anyone's contemporary sense of experience and identity. What results from this knowledge of threshold and limit is a poetry which can neither disavow (ignore) nor name (identify) subconscious linkages. These are poems which, ordinarily using the materials of everyday experience, upset meanings which would otherwise resolve into clearly interpretable symbols and images.

***

Hart might be described, then, as a poet whose ordinary way of conceiving the world poetically is via a latent and atmospherically sensitive way of responding to it. If there is a major distinction to be drawn here between his work and many others', it lies in his propensity towards invoking this heightened, implicitly intuitive awareness as a form of poetic imagination different from what we normally mean by the term. This is an imagination which is not, if the paradox can be admitted, imaginative and which lacks many of the obvious identifying traits of poetic imagining. It lacks, for instance, a resolved vision, a clearness of image. It often lacks what Pound meant by the phanopoeic, visualising area of mind and language, a visibly articulated narrative drive. Hart instead is a poet of latent, reverie-like states of mind and feeling, producing a poetry unlike the poetry which resolves into atomised moments of sensation. He is not someone who paints in words or takes photographs of pictures in the mind, letting them find their own ironic placement in time and loss. In fact, Hart could even be described as a poet who lacks the explosive "imagination" which poets ordinarily have. Drawing on an impetus connected with dream state and reveries, the imaginal zone he works from is fluid and shape shifting, building a sense of a world never free from the ghost of psyche or self awareness. Hart's manner is to portray a sense-of or a feeling-for a thing rather than an image of it, and to offer a style of perception already suffused with a reflection on its own intentionality. The images we find in his poetry are never meant to achieve what Wallace Steven's once called the definiteness of the "bright, obvious", given that the world he is representing is constantly at the edge of language or utterance.[46]

At the same time, this imaginal zone is for Hart that state of mind where the capacity to invoke images appears as a kind of compulsive "core" drive, whether it is experienced as dream-state or semi-conscious impulse or everyday experience or

46 Wallace Stevens, *The Collected Poems*, Alfred A Knopf, New York, 1981, p 351

nameless desire. Such latently imaginal states occur, in other words, only in the here-and-now as part of the particularity of *this* instant, *this* sense, *this* experience, while at the same time they open up manifold connections and emotional histories which lie in and around that moment. In this state, the words to describe what is sensed flicker on the tip of the tongue and never fully account for one's experience. Like a momentary state of mind seemingly next to (not fully spoken by) language and accordingly akin to atmosphere, his poems which capture this mode often carry a remembered and intuitive sense of the world. This quality of active remembrance makes a poet so spare with biographical details, a poet so transparent in his phrasing and yet so unassertive and self effacing as Hart is, come over to the reader as a writer who writes with an extraordinary intimacy of feeling and tone. He seems to write not just from inside his own state of mind and feeling, but also from inside ours.

The emotional core of Hart's poems, however, is not only one which lies beyond the limits of language in an external sense. It is also that zone which lies in a psychoanalytic way too deeply within utterance, too bound up within intimate drive and mood for a line, an image or a symbol to be ever more than provisionally and partially described. All names can be washed away as the Pacific Ocean's is. Both early and late work share this preoccupation with an other beyond naming. "The Street", an early prose poem, starts simply enough as a memory: "A long dark street in the east end of London" are its opening words. Rapidly, however, this memory is revealed as part of a dream scene, a kind of filmic moment in which Hart is walking down a nightmarish suburban street, peering in at the windows. A new order of provisionality enters the poem. He is in a film, he says, a "poorly made and rather sentimental" film at that. Time is somehow suspended; imaginal zones cross over into each other. For in fact (but how do we test that?) Hart says:

> I am of course walking through a vast exhibit in a museum, made larger
> than life so that its point will not be missed by even the most cursory
> visitor [...] At the end of the street I see the full moon which doubles as a
> clock for the entire museum. It tells me that it is much later than I had
> thought, that I have stayed too long, that the museum is closed and I am
> locked in for the night. Nothing to do now but wait until morning, as all
> these dead have been waiting for years.[47]

By the same token certain "scenes", certain senses, constantly repeat as if they are effects of a steady subliminal pressure. These scenes constitute a series of attractors or emotional "centres" operating over the field of the poetry's imaginal levels, becoming the themes and tones which, like endlessly fruitful mythemes, he re-awakens in poem after poem. They are the zones of the dream, the family, the shadow, the childhood memory, the summer, the clock, the moon, the face, the sun, the garden, the line of hills, the night time fear. He rings changes upon these zones throughout the many years' work. Subjected to the play of a kind of mythic infancy – subjected, that is, to a creative figure of the *in-fans,* the speaking and not-speaking, the one who hears and does not speak – these common enough images work like constantly malleable tokens which transact the familiarity of everyday experience and the mystery of the "something else", of the unspoken and of the subvocal drive. They carry the extra-linguistic energy of things and feelings.

---

47 Hart, op cit, p 26

who wants to create Australia?

Hart is often talked about by critics as primarily a religious poet. It is true that you cannot read his work without following through the connections he makes between the post-mortem condition of his imaginal world and his sustained reflection on the dreamscape and the deathscape. There are many such death poems, sometimes written with a kind of gallows humour, sometimes written in a state of ageing anxiety and sometimes written, as a *redivivus* Metaphysical poet might do, on the question of his shadow's transparency. Hart is alone among contemporary Australian poets in making the traditional theme of *memento mori* (handed down via Chaucer, Herrick, Herbert and Keats) entirely his own; and he does so, in one sense, quite against the temper of these nearly ex-post-modern times. Death becomes for him another boundary, another limit in the relations between experience and language where that adventure of desire, that "energy", undergoes its nameless, grief-struck transformation.

More profoundly, however, death references like these are symptoms of a figure which, less literally handled, are widely and sometimes secretly inflected by a number of contemporary philosophical preoccupations. It is of course some such set of themes drawn from the house of absence that has controlled a powerful current in criticism and language philosophy over the past two decades. Hart is explicit about his links with such ideas in late poems like "Approaching Sleep" where he writes a letter to god who sends it back, changing the meaning of everything said in the letter. In this poem, whose theme operates in a way which would not be unfamiliar to a reader of Derrida, writing and reading are envisaged as being controlled by a primary absence, firstly by the absence of a name (an address) for god and secondly by the way the writer's voice is subsumed and cancelled by the unconscious, self-reflexive "writing" of the literary text (the letter is sent back.) "The Map" is another such poem. A suburban family opens a map of death which (as the notion of philosophical "thought" does) depicts everything in the world. The problem is that the family discover that they do not know how to fold the map up again, "the map" being now the whole project of thinking, mapping and dying.

Perhaps a more sustained, and more overt poem of this kind is "Reading at Evening". Its night time theme and its spooks could easily suggest the influence of Wallace Stevens's major poems on reading; but it is, quite contrarily, a nihilistic refutation of the American poet's re-creative vision of reading. For Stevens, reading was a type of primary imaginative power. In Hart's hands, the book is no longer Stevens's book of mind and nature but a book which proves merely "that books do not exist". As he finishes reading, he discovers the night time world is merely looking back ironically at him through the eyes of his cat which is busily chasing its tail. The book may continue:

> ...brilliant to the end,
> and then, at midnight, the clock adds its applause.
> Outside, the cat is chasing its own tail.[48]

It is a moment of futility and self mockery.

Whatever their differences, the comparison with Stevens is not inappropriate. Every significant poet thinks about the nature of reading, not as an external matter of

---

48 Hart, op cit, p 148

literary comment of the "Who did you read last week?" variety but as something built into the very structure of the poem. In this regard an earlier poem of Hart's, "The Horizon", becomes one of the key poems of his work. It anticipates and encapsulates many of the themes about language and absence which occur in the later poetry. In this poem, too, a devotional intent and a reflection on the structural nature of writing cannot be disassociated. Like "Dark Angel" and "Facing the Pacific at Night", this is a poem about boundaries, about knowledges on the other side of perception. It is about the state of mind and feeling where you sense you are being unconsciously spoken to. Long ago it might have indicated that if he is a religious poet focussed on the deathscape, this is not so in any simple sense: in "The Horizon" the terms of death, limit and readability have already become inextricable.

Thus the horizon acts quite literally as the threshold boundary over which a back-of-the-mind voice starts to speak, addressing the reader directly until towards the end of the poem it is saying:

> You who hate departures,
> You who forever try to shut me out
> Listen to me:
> Whenever you think of death,
> Whenever you enter the room of someone gone from you,
> I will be peering through the window.
> I will catch you
> Even though my net has just one string.
> You have no need for mirrors
> Who lie to you until it is too late...[49]

Stanza by stanza, Hart moves through the various unnamed "names" of the limit which such a horizon places on distance and eyesight: the horizon becomes, for example, the dividing line between the conscious, visible world and the "whole" hidden world which is both on the other side of the horizon and at the same time beneath it:

> You see only the top line of my head
> Beneath that I have the world
> With all its fields sun moonlight and rain.[50]

It is as if the game of naming need never cease. For the horizon speaks also as The Comforter, observing the priest about his rituals ("The old priest hurrying to mass"); then it speaks as the naked, revealed thing invisible to those who cannot bear "to see me as I truly am". Whatever construction is put upon it, it puts a break into experience. It introduces a fracture between the known "here" and the unknown "there". It speaks back and responds to the position of the viewer. It cannot help but challenge us, as Hart puts it in the final lines, to look at it and

> ... see the only truth
> Your past what you are now
> All your future sorrows and your only blessing.[51]

---

49 op cit, p 22
50 ibid
51 op cit, p 23

Arguably, this horizon is a key underlying figure in Hart's poetry. It defines the kind of re-creative space that the particularity of his poetry and its imaginal zones introduce into experience. All the time, too, it is clear that whatever set of changes Hart rings on the horizon, whether the event-horizon of relativistic measurement or the temporal horizon of phenomenological experience or the convergent perspective of God's presence in the world, the horizon is something which the viewer reads and which reads the viewer. "The Horizon", like many other of his poems, is an expansion on this figure of reading, not just in terms of how we find the horizon to be a naturally inescapable limit on what can be scanned and felt but also in terms of how it puts artificial definitions and limits on our experience. The horizon sets up the dimensions of above and below, here and there, inside and outside, visibility and invisibility which his best poems always work with. As a fracture and limit, it imposes the edge of what anyone can know via language. It instantly suggests that, while there is a complete freedom to travel towards and away from that horizon, it is not possible ever to be free of the way it produces itself as the comforter or as a frontier between the living and the dead or as the boundary between truth and dream. This horizon is a break or literal limit on thought and vision; it works as the boundary round the core imaginal zones of each of his finest poems. It blocks utterance and yet its voice can always be heard. It is both an *a*ffect and an *e*ffect of position.

Hart's poems work like these horizons. They are not spiritual exercises nor Pascalian thoughts to be elucidated and internalised. The imaginal zones which his poetry works with might well constitute in the eyes of some readers the groundwork, the potential earth, out of which the plant of blossoming faith can spring. But in distinction to this way of reading him, I would suggest that his poems offer a carefully undercut psychological space within the horizon of experience, a space which can always be read and felt at different levels. This space is constantly played over by subliminal voices whether they are formed by the poet's sense of an unspeaking and an unspoken dimension to his experiences or whether they are the familiar, ghostly memories of past anxiety or future pleasure. In this way, his poetry defines a particularly contemporary kind of psyche, one which is not inert in relation to a perennial matter at the centre of the connections between poetic language and ontology, between imagining and describing. His voice situates itself within a broader understanding of contemporary poetics whilst staying true to poetry's everyday, concretely referenced dimensions.

A horizon is also a figure of judgment. For no less than in the case of the therapeutic narratives of psychoanalysis, the exploration of what was earlier termed the imaginal area of the psyche stands itself under a figure of interpretation, an interpretation to do with the completeness of the rendition and the level of precision with which the poet can define the status of the experience encountered in each poem. It is the judgment of where you stand. There is a genuine truth-factor here which prevents Hart's poetry from ever being reduced to a mere mythology of the everyday self. This lack of self might even suggest a direct link with Freud and his descendants, whose explorations of imaginal areas were always cast under the light of that most enlightened yet intangible ideal: to experience and act towards each other in a self realising way and to be free of neurosis. No less, the theme of selflessness connects Hart's work with one of the major aims of a philosopher like Derrida who proposes a vision of experience both simple and powerful. Namely, that we should be able to understand both the highs and the lows, both the conscious and unconscious meanings of language and of experience without recourse to any form of that over-riding "name", that "surname" (whether god, nation, language, soul, poetry, land) which Hart seeks to free himself from in "Facing the Pacific at Night". The clarity, beauty and intelligence of Hart's work, its simplicity and its modern range, make his poetry of commanding interest. His poems speak from the zone of the "nameless one" of truly achieved writing. Who knows what transformation he will work on his faces, his shadows, his clocks, his moons and future landscapes, his summers and night time anxiety, in the coming years? One cannot help but think that it will be a magic transmutation, a re-reading and re-siting, of the deepest themes.

self, place, newness[52]

*H*istorically, Australian poetry has articulated a distinctively complex set of relationships with the British and American traditions and yet in an international perspective it is the one of these three national literatures which has been largely overlooked. At the same time, though our poetry has always been readable both with and differently from those foreign literatures, few writers or critics have chosen to make that sameness and difference a matter of critical importance. The tendency has been that a nationalist promotion of Australian poetry just takes for granted that somehow the work should be better known overseas. Examples where these critical and literary connections are made explicit such as Tom Shapcott's 1976 anthology, *Contemporary American and Australian Poetry,* are rare. The carefully employed international and philosophical framework which is present in American critic and poet Paul Kane's survey *Australian Poetry: Romance and Negativity* is even rarer.[53]

Another American critic, Nicholas Birns, has more recently addressed the same issue, suggesting that Australian literature upsets what he terms the "paralysing British-American dichotomy" not least because its themes and its historical periods differ from British and American ones and are often incommensurable with the well-worn categories through which English language literary critical history is usually written.[54] Yet when we turn to recent poetry, Australian poetry's presence overseas adds up to more than what we have seen so many times before – the culturally colonising centres of London, New York and Paris discovering a new exotic literature which they then celebrate, import for a few years and then forget all about – we must also be able to say something more precise about in what that newness (and interestingness) consist. Put plainly: *why* is recent Australian poetry different from the poetry of English and American poets writing contemporarily? If it is different, why should the work of our poets make any wider claims upon a general readership than, say, the work of a gifted poet from California or a new voice from Lancashire?

The issue has some urgency. As the critical context for modern Australian poetry grows wider, it is important to be able to answer those questions in a way which deals closely with the ideas and themes of the poets and which does not just beat drums. One of these ideas, for instance, is the connection between post-modern and post-

---

52 First pubished in *Meanjin, Poetics,* 2/ 2001

53 Ed. Thomas Shapcott, *Contemporary American and Australian Poetry*, University of Queensland Press, Brisbane, 1976; Paul Kane, *Australian Poetry: Romance and Negativity*, Cambridge University Press, Cambridge, 1996.

54 Nicholas Birns, "May in September: Australian Literature as Anglophone Alternative" in ed. David Callahan, *Contemporary Issues in Australian Literature*, Frank Cass, London and Portland 2002 p 113 passim

colonial ideas about culture and place and identity (especially in critical theory in the northern hemisphere) and what can perhaps too readily be identified as a recurrent pre-occupation with self and place in Australian poetry. What may not be so apparent to the overseas reader interested in such ideas is that this is a traditional theme stretching back to colonial times. It is not just a contemporary matter. Nonetheless, that reader may turn out to be well served in updating the theme and identifying it as also a post-modern concern located in a repertoire of ideas to do with subjectivity, the environment and the senses.

Perhaps this is to say no more than that a necessary re-contextualisation takes place. So, when British critic Jonathan Bate speaks of the particularity of the "bioregional emphasis" in Les Murray's poetry, his is a transformative reading which situates Murray in the context of Wordsworth, Gary Snyder and Basil Bunting. For Bate, Murray is "the major ecological poet currently writing in the English language."[55] Such a judgement draws attention to the poet's birth-country. But a no less vital context for Bate's insightful claim is the lively interest in the relationship between poetics and the environment amongst readers and critics all over the world. Bate is obviously right in implying that the significant meanings which can be attached to Murray's particular "bioregional emphasis" (the bush, the North Coast) are global as well as Australian.

Similarly it makes sense to say that Australian poetry is different from the work of many (not all) modern American and British writers because a disproportionately large number of Australian poets intuit that the theme of local feeling, place and placement is important to them and their readers. What such poetry deals with is not just a feeling about landscape or land in a romantic or nostalgic way. One thing indeed that sets Australian work apart is a prevalent sense that "country" (definitely not countryside, nearly yet not quite what Americans and Europeans call land and landscape) is something you are a part of, something which changes your senses of self and placement and which requires a change in envisioning if you are to see it and understand it. Land, in other words, is active and malleable; it can also be oneiric and ancestral; while, as if in contradiction to those largely symbolic facets of a sense of place, many of the discussions and sentiments best associated with country are technical, environmental and technological matters, in part discontinuous from human images and uses of it. Besides, country does not easily offer back a comfortable image of white Western presence, neither in terms of colonial history nor in terms of technological intervention and environmental degradation. This obliges anyone writing about Australian poetry to recognise that a claim about the wider contemporaneity of Australian poetry must reflect a fairly high level of discontinuity: the claim is that almost inevitably in a specifically Australian relationship between poetry and place you will find a profound but at the same time a fragmented sense of subject and land.

That disjunctive sense of place is what the following five critical sketches seek to explore. To be disjunctive, it must be emphasised, is not the same as being ironic or merely negative. At the back of each set of notes there was also the question of what makes the variety, and what forms the commonality, in the way these poets identify themselves and their feelings in, and to do with, place. Since one of the poets was not born or brought up in Australia and one has spent little of his adult life here, the stress

---

55 Jonathan Bate, *The Song of the Earth*, Harvard University Press, Cambridge 2000, p 238

MARTIN HARRISON

Dear Jonathan Plater,

It is a real privilege to be able to send you some of my essays. I hope there are some resonances with your own writing on place and environment.

With all best wishes,

Martin H

POSTAL: 'SHANTIPUR', CANNING STREET, WOLLOMBI,
NEW SOUTH WALES 2325, AUSTRALIA

E-MAIL: **martinh@hunterlink.net.au**   PH/FAX: (61 2) 4998 3228

too is definitely on being in place, not about place or from place. Nor is there any contention that what results is conclusive or exhaustive, even if hopefully the overlaps (no less than the absence of certain areas of pre-occupation) are certainly of interest. All the poems were published between 1975 and 1990, a period which generally was reflective of a higher level of attentiveness to what Philip Hodgins back then called 'landspeak' than might be the case now. If recent Australian poetry has something new to say, and especially says it newly to non-Australians, then it will (among other considerations) derive from what is captured in the self reflective, closely felt and technologically aware engagement of our poets to place and environment.

1. Jennifer Rankin's *"Old Currawong"*

What makes Jennifer Rankin's poem "Old Currawong" so unforgettable is the way in which it both emphasises time and also suspends it, freezing time-flow in an image which is neither memory nor up-front fact. What makes it distinctive is the attention given to a relatively unusual phenomenon, rain :

> After the sudden rain
> the heavy after-drops still thudding
>
> a large black currawong still slipping
> gripping rasping in the corrugations of the iron roof
>
> and the lorikeets flying in only as colour
> and the talking of the koels and the crows circling above
>
> I see the black neck stretching
> the opening beak the awkward sliding feet
>
> always unbalancing trying to regain to stand up straight
>
> while the great heavy weight of the body
> slips on and over the roof
>
> The last of the rain falls hard and separate and of its own
>
> But the beak of the bird is still there high on the roof.
>
> Yes the beak is still there pinned to the iron ridge.
>
> I see it open I see the long dark shaft of the beak open
>
> From deep below the earth it pulls out its cry.[56]

Here, very precise details, the thud of rain drops after the rain has stopped, the scratching sounds of the bird on the corrugated metal roof, suggest a singular and exact moment cut across by the flight of lorikeets and the sound of crows. Many things happen in this poem, each isolated in their own packet of time.

"Old Currawong" is, however, a poem in which movement matters as much as stillness. Though each event is isolated in time, nothing rests, nothing is inert. Rain drops fall; the currawong slips on the roof; high up, the warning crows circle; the bird unbalances; it cannot retain a grasp on the ground; its beak opens and the cry is pulled out. "Old Currawong" is a poem whose key figure is a figure of instability and transience, no less than it is a poem where there is an increasing intensification of focus and attentiveness. The poem cannot help but suggest, as so much Australian landscape

---

56 Jennifer Rankin, *Collected Poems*, ed Judith Rodriguez, University of Queensland Press, Brisbane, 1990, p 217

does, the intensity of the singular and relatively minimal event occurring in a context (whether an air, a weather, a spaciousness) which is both huge and indifferent. In such immensity, the act of seeing, the act of responding become all important.

This was Jennifer Rankin's way. In her seeing there is always a space around things. There is always more, a something in a space-beyond, which cannot be taken into account. Rather, wherever you are, you are conscious of space as the medium through which things move. Space and thing have a flat, dynamic, aerial relationship: "the sky," as she puts it in another poem, " is loosened. / We watch it bleed into the sea."[57] Or again, when gauging the way a rock or the flight of a bird *stand out* in space:

> I am not speaking of shadow.
> I speak of the line. Butting and carving.
> And again of the line. Edging the air. [58]

Always, however, that sense of the line comes home, so to speak, as an internalised sense of what is around her. Even when her eyes are closed, even when not paying attention: "I close my eyes and the line rolls in and under my lids." This sense of a space-beyond is not represented or thought about in the way a European writer might do it; which is to say, it is not constructed as a static optical context or visual background or a move between foreground and middleground within the field of Renaissance perspective. Rankin tangibly grasps the power of earth and air: she is their poet. In poem after poem, her work demonstrates her understanding of the specificity that sky and ground have in a flat, spacious country. Her vision has been rethought (in much the way painters often have to think out an "idea" of seeing) both philosophically and bodily.

We could think of Rankin as a poet who literalises the nature of country, both earth and air, in a feminine way which the philosopher Irigaray has recently described as that way of making the world proximal and close at hand by lending one's living body as a gathering place for the whole.[59] Or we could see her as a poet who worked out her senses through a detailed understanding of the appropriateness to Australian perceptions of the flat, depthless canvases of the 60s and 70s. (Her poetry's identification with the painting of John Olsen is of paramount importance.) But more than anything she is a poet who, in a truly structural sense, understood the need to see across boundaries: a need to see her own glimpse, her own intense imagining, of local time and space as themselves mobile, temporary and temporal.

2. Robert Gray's *"The Poem"*

The line may cut through space but still make it unclear where you are facing. To be isolated is, for example, not just to be without neighbours, or proximity: it is more about not knowing in which direction you are facing. It's about being in the open, at sea whether on land or the ocean. Perhaps in the final analysis, the ground of such isolation, the emotional base of it, is a sense that wherever you are you could be facing

---

57 Rankin, op cit, "Reef Heron Fishing", p 214

58 op.cit, "The Line", p 57

59 c.f. Luce Irigaray, *The Forgetting of Air in Martin Heidegger* trans Mary Beth Mader, University of Texas, Austin, 1999, p 66: "lending her living body as a gathering place for the whole: she works only with proximity unless she prefers to rest..."

in all directions, facing an endless horizon with the demoralising feeling that it does not matter whether you go this way or that. *Open, openness, open space* are all loaded words catching more a feeling of sad vacancy than they do any Old World (or American) sense of opportunity and freedom. All too often it is precisely openness, whether of the open sky or the open plains, which has defeated and unsettled non-Indigenous Australians.

This is why the word "open" matters in "The Poem." It occurs twice, first in a description of space:

> The paddocks there are so wide open
> she says you always feel
> that the lid has been left off everything...

And, no less negatively, as a verb:

> On the backs of her hands, in this light, open
> small, dry screams...

Here, openness is a lack of necessary containment. It's the property by which things boil dry in an incessantly hot climate. It's the sign of that deep, domestic poverty in which the cooking pots do not have proper lids. Or it measures the harshness of sunlight on skin where a woman's hands prematurely age in the grinding round of family chores.

"The Poem", however, is most obviously about making poetry; and as such it takes us back to family experience and maternal experience. The central figure is a single parent in a house out nowhere, at the edges of a project home development or perhaps a house out on the plains. We feel, however, only the light skin of the house and its fragility. The light is so blindingly hot that the children have to be kept in the shade of the verandah. The woman goes outside to bring in the washing:

The Poem

> The paddocks there are so wide open
> she says you always feel
> that the lid has been left off everything.
> It's all gone hard and stale.
>
> The children have to stay in the shade;
> they hang from the verandah,
> and the game they fight about is discovering
> a demand upon her.
>
> On the backs of her hands, in this light, open
> small, dry screams.
> She is bringing in the sunlit bed-clothes,
> putting together the seams.
>
> Sheets still pegged she takes into her fist,
> and stands inhaling each one:
> taut with air, white as a heron in the moonlight.
> This, which she has done.[60]

In this environment, achievement shrinks down to the repetition of a small gesture. Similarly, to make a poem is a small, ignorable intervention in all of that openness. But

---

60 Robert Gray, *New and Selected Poems*, op cit, p 119

the woman's poem has no language. What it shares with a written work is the fact it is achieved on a human scale.

Openness, that is to say, returns you to where you are at home. It returns you to an unnoticeable ritual which is not, first and foremost, a matter of words. In fact, nothing in "The Poem" is about making poetry in the obvious sense of an educated, or cultivated, pleasure. The house faces nowhere. It is drowned in space. Much of the minimal living which goes on there has gone "hard and stale". There is a single reference to something which might offer some form of assuagement, the whiteness of a heron glimpsed on a moonlit night. (So much information about how Australian night is welcome for its coolness is expressed in that image.) And there is a sense of what might be termed a *sufficiency* even if Gray's idea of having "done" something ("This, which she has done") typifies the sort of tonal complexity for which his poetry is unsurpassed. Thus perhaps this line could read complacently. If this is so the poem ends with a simple conviction in the power of small actions, even with a possibly intentional smugness caught in the poet's over-estimation of the significance of a small repeated task. On the other hand, all action (including this poem) is placed by the poet under light of that very same idea of sufficiency and openness: it is admired and overwhelmed at one and the same time. "The Poem" describes a simple action which is beyond words and which is at once celebrated and disparaged by the immensity which surrounds it. Such a line carries an unmistakable range of local knowledge.

3. Antigone Kefala's *"Goddess"*

Is it true to say that a voice in a poem is always a particular kind of voice, a particular tone, a particular closeness or distance? The question to ask when reading Antigone Kefala's "Goddess" is who is speaking? or more precisely what sort of a voice is speaking? and where? in what region of mood and mind?

Goddess

The evening was falling
on the porcelain dust
that moved on the waters
the milky white breath
of the goddess with snakes
who travelled below
her slim arms outstretched
poised at the centre
a secretive smile
on her listening mouth.

At her feet
the octopus waited
watchful
with eyes of the deep.[61]

After all, the poem is simply an observation, someone looking at the evening light on water. "Goddess" is not strictly speaking a poem of the interior monologue voice or

61 Antigone Kefala, *Absence: New and Selected Poems*, Hale and Iremonger, Sydney, 1998, p 79

of the stream-of-consciousness voice, however intimate sounding. The tone is public, matter of fact.

This is so despite the fact that this voice is talking about an association, a link which is highly specific to that falling evening light, a particular sense of whiteness, of movement, of diffraction and depth. In every way, the poem is an observation which is built on water. What the poet sees is a shimmer show of late light on moving waves, a close-up of a sinuous momentary effect of evening sun on dark, deep waves. It's hard not to pick up the glinting, glancing quality of the goddess, the seductive body movements, the wriggles and undulations. But are we seeing anything real, out there? Is the poem operating in the here-and-now as a report on experience or is it (more likely) a kind of memory, a sense of late light brought momentarily into consciousness and thereby identified as a visual trace, whose specific time and place have been forgotten or rendered useless?

The eye and voice which can invent such vision and invent it out of such a momentarily remembered fragment can only come from a poet operating on the boundary of known and unknown areas of awareness. No-one reading "Goddess" can fail to understand the way in which the poem oscillates between tangible and intangible orders of experience. We deal with matters of fact, of perception and detailed observation no less than with matters of unconscious imagining. Where the matters of unconscious imagining are concerned, the poem offers the image of a classical statue drowned beneath the surface, much like an archaeological "find" in a submerged ancient city, some Heraklion or Atlantis. Where matters of perceived sense data predominate, we never fail to be aware that what is visible is no more than the light-flow on water and that its sinuosity provokes an echo or a responsive image in the mind. As we look lower and deeper (literally, down to the feet of the statue) so we look lower and deeper into the mind: there, in those depths, we encounter octopi, transmutations and unpredictable powers. A pattern is created between the viewing of a quasi-object (in the water) and the understanding of a specific movement of thought.

What, then, is this *specific* object of thought in the poem and what is that region of mood and mind in which this object occurs? One response is that looking into the water in "Goddess" we could be looking into the source of dreams. We could be looking, for instance, into what Gaston Bachelard called the hinge or the juncture of oceanic light where "water grasps the sky".[62] For Bachelard such water reveries were not only dreams of goddesses and sprites and beckoning undines, they were also dreams of return to home, both of a return to a house and also of a return to a home which is beyond death. "Water comes to signify," he wrote in *Water and Dreams*, "that most distant of homes, a celestial one."[63]

Water and water images cathect at such deep levels, indeed, that there is even a certain risk in this matter of looking into water, a fear that the ruffled water will go still, transparently reflective and deathly. To quote Bachelard again, this danger results from the fact that water can give an absolute reflection of where we are now when we look. "In so pure a mirror," he wrote, "the world is my vision." Certainly it's

---

62 Gaston Bachelard, *Water and Dreams*, trans Edith Farrell, Dallas Institute of Humanities and Culture, Dallas, 1983, p 48ff.

63 ibid

the place, mythic, no doubt, that we would like to return to in Kefala's poem. In "Goddess", it is an absent place which the poet is mesmerised by, indeed almost mocked by in the way that a seductive, naked woman might mock her lover as a form of provocation.

Mind, thought, feeling are caught in a moment of passage, a moment in between. Kefala is the poet of this style of absence, of a beyond momentarily caught in mind and lost as soon as reflected on. "Goddess" is a recollection of how the figure of divinity emerges from the water. This light-on-water hovers somewhere between percept and a form of mythic identification. It is about naming and about both the loss and the evocation of a spirit in place.

4. Peter Porter's *"An Australian Garden"*

Talking from, talking beyond and around a thing: what is referred to in the poem's title, "An Australian Garden", immediately begins to fluctuate in a game of different connotations, a game which exploits the different usages and meanings a phrase can have. After all, an "Australian garden" is a colonial phrase – colonial because we can immediately sense the extra meaning of putting in that word "Australian", as if something about an immediate reality (the reality of gardens, for instance) has permanently to be qualified as being defiantly Australian, at odds with, or definable in contrast to, a non-Australian inheritance. We are not just talking about gardens; nor do we want this locally specific sense of the garden to be confused with "English" gardens or "French" gardens.

In its very layout Porter's garden is paradoxical. A reader notices the formality of his poem and the absence of a sense of wilderness, of surrounding mountains, or of the garden being bounded by a nature which is not-garden. In the same way, there is no pioneering sense of this area being inhabited by an isolated individual who, Thoreau-like, tends his beans and cuts strides of wood by the log cabin's front door. No bush, no forest, no native wilderness surround and swamp this Australian colonial garden space. The paradox is that it is the garden itself which seems wild, riotous and without boundary. In fact, does this garden have a boundary, a wall or a hedge? As a space, this Australian garden offers no contrast between cultivated, formal terrain and a wild 'outside' in the way that, for instance, an Arabic garden might do; nor, though we can guess that it is in a city, is there any contrast made between the garden's reclusive, tranquil space and a dense, noisy, polluted urban environment.

It lacks a clear external boundary perhaps for no better reason than that none is acknowledged. But Peter Porter's Australian garden equally has no *inner* boundaries. It is a space where a number of eclectic mythological and poetic references accumulates in a higgledy piggledy manner. It can be an Eden where "we enact the opening of the world" no less than it is a childhood memory, a Dantean wood, a dream garden, a paradigm for the mix of foreign and native species; or it can be a place where we simply become conscious of the lack of water works and classical statuary in the Baroque manner. You can talk about anything you like in this Australian garden: it is a space which lends itself to short poetic divagations, to cleverness and to verbal exercises upon the eclectic nature it contains. What is equally sure is that to make meaning from its bizarrely displaced elements requires a very accomplished level of verbal style, a style which can weave between and across these elements, not fastening on them too often or with too intense a gaze.

Gardens have traditionally been the place for naming things. However, in Peter Porter's Australian garden (and in similar of his poems) you can only be aware that language cannot name absolutely. Names can be swapped and changed and paraphrased. This seems to be the price you pay for the playful and delightful eclecticism which the garden expresses. It is as if an excess of naming (too many things, too many names) ultimately undermines or ironises the purpose and value of the activity. Words go so far and no further and are never able to express adequately what the writer means them to say. The instability of names is also obviously at the heart of the failure of art to satisfy the creator's (the artist's, the divine artist's) intentions. This is how Porter describes this necessary 'failure' in all art work in another poem, this time set in Italy, but equally to do with an artificial natural space like the Australian garden. In "At Lake Massaciuccoli," Porter writes of how the artist knows that:

> No one produces the art he wants to,
> Everything that he makes is code,
> To be read for its immaculate intention.
> Then in death he finds the final disappointment,
> That no clarity comes anywhere, the perfect
> Vision has gone into the mist, as when dawn
> Wakens the wet-winged skimmers on the lake
> And every hazy lineament lures the hunter
> Into a picture-postcard world...[64]

The will to express an "immaculate intention" can only be understood ironically. Even when you encounter the perfect vision on the perfect morning, what you look at immediately resembles something represented: an idyllic shot on a postcard, for example. Only the best of intentions are what you are left with. Or perhaps you are just left with the postcards. So too in "An Australian Garden" it would, says Porter, be "easy to unimagine everything."

There is a fleetingness too about this garden. You must not linger over any specific moment, any haunting view, if you are to be able to understand the whole of the place. The individual elements are simply too disjoined, and have too complex individual histories, to pause over. Each of them (the childhood angophora, the perfectibility of wind-noise in trees, the deep roots of the camellias) will take you off-track and require an excessive amount of post-colonial qualification if you decide to focus closely on them and think their existence through.

Not surprising, then, what strikes the imagination in this garden is not so much the flowers and the animals but a moment of weather change when the heat cools and a southerly blows in. It is often the case at the end of a blindingly hot January day around Sydney. So too in Porter's poem:

> In the afternoon we change – an afterthought,
> Those deeper greens which join the stalking shadows –
> The lighter wattles look like men of taste
> With a few well-tied leaves to brummel-up

---

64 Porter, op cit, p 306

Their poise. Berries dance in a southerly wind
And the garden tide has turned. Dark on dark.
Janus leaves are opening to the moon
Which makes its own grave roses. Old Man
Camellias root down to keep the sun intact,
The act is canopied with stars. A green sea
Rages through the landscape all the night.

Similarly, if everything in this variegated space can be spoken about, then that is so only because each object is treated with a degree of superficiality. We can see and pay attention to objects provided that we acknowledge that what presents itself *first* to our eyes are the highlights and the glitter. Only then what we see engages our capacity to make language. Even the enigmatic moment of mood, the shift of temperature and wind which constitute a play of light in dark and dark in light, are themselves detachable from the complex, overlaid regiments of plants and spaces. That sense of traces flashing and building and unbuilding is why, in a marvellous image of oncoming dusk, "nondescript pinks/ Survive the death of light." This Australian garden is a necessarily disjoined consciousness.

So *anything* can be said. We do not need to know the depth of the illusion. What is allowed in Australia is a playfulness which could more or less detach itself from any need to keep referencing and to keep dealing with the known real world: such play leads to a poetry so allusive and fast it becomes largely abstract, expressing an aesthetic playfulness whose tendency is towards an ultimate play of signifiers. This is a poetry which is so perplexed, so silenced, by the difficulty of accounting for local history (that riotous inter-connectedness of so many growing forms) that it has to become ahistorical. Everything which is said has to be said self-reflexively, abstractly. Every thing is named here and now, and yet is named only provisionally, only *for* the here and now.

There is a constant pressure in our poetry towards this writing of immediate surface reference (and ultimately of a de-referenced abstraction) felt in more or less every epoch of modern Australian poetry: it starts with Brennan, but it is found in work as diverse as the Angry Penguins, John Tranter, John Forbes and it is currently reappearing as the current Language-school influence on many of today's younger poets. The poetic imagination is not constructed according to the rules of a Renaissance water garden in Italy, nor according to the heavenly glimpses of a water-mirrored Moghul garden any more than it is by Walden Pond in the New England woods. Where is the water, Porter asks:

...where the terraces, the Tritons
And the cataracts of moss? This is Australia
And the villas are laid out inside their eyes...

5. Philip Hodgins' "The Discs"

All of the above poems are poems about time out, time out of occupation, time out of thought, time momentarily released from chores, like the mother figure in Robert Grey's poem. Very few poems in any language successfully celebrate, or even comment on, work: Raymond Carver is close to this theme in poems like "The Autopsy Room" and "Powder-Monkey" and another highly accomplished American poet, Philip Levine, often memorialises his own experiences of industrial work and fellow factory workers. Work is usually, however, where the poetic imagination is not: in Carver's phrase work is where "in the end you are totally crushed".[65] But Philip Hodgins wrote quite a number of poems which are about work, including some of his best poems – poems like "Chopped Prose with Pigs," "Second Thoughts on the Georgics", "Superphosphate" and "Three Pig Diseases". Even in a late poem like "A House in the Country", it is the attention to the detail of physical labour which most impresses. Very few poets can render so exactly what it is like to prize a wall apart with a jemmy in pursuit of white ants, effortlessly demonstrating that the writer also knows the studs, noggins, bearers and tin-caps he encounters. True, most readers of Hodgins will read this poem as, to some degree, a metaphor for a body dying of cancer, but it is written by someone who seems to have had a direct experience of house building and carpenting and who is unafraid of talking unaffectedly and knowledgeably about physical work.

Given his country background, many of the physical tasks reported on in Hodgins are farm work. Fencing, milking, baling, the handling and killing of animals (this last is often treated graphically), woodchopping, the seemingly endless round of land and home maintenance jobs which proliferate on properties: all these work-themes are in Hodgins' poetry. Mostly, as with the house building example, there is a sense that his attentiveness to the nature of these activities was not just the fruit of external observation: the descriptions of equipment and its uses are too meticulous for that, as is the intuitive way in which he gives an account of how a worker is articulated in movement while working. In other contexts, too, his poems often capture the exactness of how someone stands or how someone thinks in movement. So, for instance, a man leaning on a rail, contemplating slaughtering his herd of diseased pigs, realises that even the rail will have to be burnt and then:

> ...stabs with a boot
> into the dirt, which will have to be treated.[66]

Similarly, a simple but wonderfully observed moment in a hunting trip contains these expertly understood movements as a young girl walks back to the ute and her father searches for bullets in the glove box:

> ...On her way back she looked across
> the paddocks to a silver square of light
> reflecting from a roof, the galvo slopes
> of home, and thought about the swallows there.
> Len hadn't found the bullets. "Shit," she heard
> him say. She watched him rummaging as if
> he had to find his licence for a cop.
> A couple of galahs went overhead.[67]

Spaciousness, time, the isolatedness of human gesture and interaction, the construction of distance and closeness through vehicles, the way events (like the galahs flying through) are etched into time, the futility and clumsiness of many utilitarian actions like rummaging in the glove-box: Hodgins has this filmic ability of describing locale and human figures as they move around "in process" and transect

---

65 Raymond Carver, *Kafka's Watch in All of Us: The Collected Poems*, The Harvill Press, London, 1996, p 182

66 Philip Hodgins, *New Selected Poems*, Duffy & Snellgrove, Sydney, 2000, p 151

67 Hodgins, *Selected Poems*, Angus and Robertson, Sydney, 1997, p 239

real atmospheres. Against the tendency to make Australian country fit within the picture frame or the long-shot, Hodgins' work makes it manifest that there is no such thing as a purely abstract faculty of seeing; there is only a way of seeing which is part and parcel of moving and doing.

"The Discs" is one of these poems of work and movement. This is how the poem opens.

> To go back purposefully to the big machinery shed
> and start the tractor up,
> and then reverse the tractor over to 'The Discs'
> enmeshed in long grass there beside the diesel tank,
> and hitch them to hydraulic sway-bars
> taking care to snap the safety-pins in place.
>
> To travel slowly down the bottom lane
> and feel the steering light and ineffectual
> because of all that weight held up behind,
> and to hear loose steel crash awkwardly
> through each dry pothole, dip
> or stretch of corrugation smudged with gravel dust.
>
> To come to a chained five-bar gate and stop
> and swing down off the tractor in one sharp movement
> landing with a crunch on Rossi workboots,
> and then to swing the gate wide open
> and stand there for a moment
> looking thoughtfully at thirty acres of rested soil.
>
> To drive into the paddock then
> and drop the discs down heavily into the dirt,
> fix the self-adjusting height control
> and set off in the lowest ratio
> with the throttle pulled back halfway,
> the engine and the discs complaining noisily.[68]

It is a detailed account of someone backing up a tractor, hitching it to one of those ploughs with a double bar of discs and driving it down the edge of a paddock (you "feel the steering light and ineffectual/ because of all that weight held up behind"), and then working around the paddock from the edge to the centre, turning its surface into loosened and plantable soil. By the end, even the tractor driver cannot avoid looking back on the work, glimpsing there a kind of mandala. In the final stanza the tractor driver thinks to himself:

> To finish just on dark
> with teal ducks going overhead towards the swamp
> and gently angled lines of dense sunlight
> investigating perfect rows of upturned soil
> that all lead ineluctably
> back into the centre of the rich paddock.

The view is an image of thirty acres of earth turned and waiting. Yet the manifest sense of satisfaction is disturbed, not as tranquil as it appears. There is the detailing of how the light is like an outside source "investigating" the paddock and there is the

---

68 Hodgins, *New Selected Poems*, op cit, p 121

reference to the ineluctability of the grooves back to the centre. The first image, the light-image, is an image of exposure; the second image of the ploughed lines' vortex is an image of time, of a focus on a particular spot in the earth (a grave?) and of spent energy. The stanza captures exactly the mix of satisfaction and tentativeness which physical achievement often leaves you with: a sense that a good, pleasurable job symbolises not just pure, physical achievement but also impermanent and spent power.

Peter Porter's harbourside garden had at its centre a sense of pleasure and playfulness to do with love. His garden of exotics and gum trees is a place for people to undergo transformations; it's a place, as he put it, to find your proper skin, to be seduced, to fall for the monster. Hodgins' paddock is no garden in this sense. It is, however, a place of intense cultivation, not least symbolically. It is a place where desire and male physical strength are exercised.

The poem has in this regard a number of paradoxes in it. After all, "The Discs" is written in the form of a series of infinitives. Each stanza starts with one of them: *to go back purposefully, to travel slowly, to come to a chained five-bar gate, to drive into the paddock then, to stay there through the day* and so on. The effect is a hesitation about whether the poem describes a task completed or a wish list of what he intends to do. "The Discs" plays these ambiguities to the full: "to go back purposefully" can be interior command, or wish or just ticking off down a list. Besides, why does the poem open so pointedly with a line about purposefulness?

To go back purposefully to the big machinery shed...

Purposefully? Was the poet putting off the task, bracing himself for it like a swimmer diving into cold water, or is he indicating that the whole activity is merely wishful thinking, merely something he can fantasise himself doing? If this latter interpretation is correct, the poem details a state of imaginary robustness and a desire to be well. The question is left disturbingly and deliberately unresolved. Even here, only a disjoined and tentative consciousness relates the poet to the earth. Hodgins is no exception to the way in which Australian poetry emerging in the context of a late modernist or post-modernist aesthetics inevitably looks beyond the natural and Nature, whether to the movement of thought, or to the movement of language or to the instability of the human construction of land and landscape.

Yet the heart of the matter is not just the manner in which a hidden figure of death undercuts an idealised image of work. It is worth bringing back to mind what an accurate sense of physical labour there is in all of Hodgins' poems. Thirty acres is a sizeable area. Turning the soil in that thirty acres requires a very long, gruesome day on a noisy tractor: worse, the labour expended is entirely machinic.[69] The clockwise way of proceeding with the land is, similarly, abstract and vehicular. The work is entirely to do with manipulating gears. Such work is a superior and exhausting form of lawn-mowing, without much connection to meditation or to nature observation. The last stanza (the one quoted above with its lovely references to the teal and the late light) captures a moment of silence as the ears clear from the engine noise. What the driver

---

69 There may also be more evidence here that the idea of ploughing these thirty acres should not be taken literally. My information is that even with the largest discs, a heavy tractor and a broad flat paddock, a long day might not be enough for that size of acreage.

self, place, newness

looks back at is a contouring which reflects machine-made senses of space and alignment. Perhaps it was to bring this element to the fore which ultimately persuaded Hodgins at the end of his life to change the title of the poem. In his *Selected Poems* he republished it under the title given here as "The Discs". Originally (and significantly) it was called "A Prayer", a reference no doubt to the repetitive and often seemingly meaningless way in which, when everything is against us, we meditate and imagine and hope.

3

After modernity, what?

James McAuley

modernity: five fragments [70]
a point of convergence

*M*odernity – the word immediately sounds over-worked and over-politicised – has been a powerful obsession in Australian aesthetics. It is a concept which links in with numerous aspects of the way a sense of local reality is represented; it often determines too the kind of relationship Australians have with overseas art-movements and overseas intellectualism and philosophy, particularly when the modern idea or style are seen as what comes from overseas in contrast to out-of-date local experience and events. In historical terms, it remains right up to today a concept reguarly deployed as a powerful ideological tool in the discourses of settlement, technological development, economic reform, globalisation and international relations. Like many ideas which are almost unmanageable in definitional terms, ideas such as "identity", "nationhood", "Australian", the theme of modernity constitutes a long-lived historical narrative of controversies and divisions. For it must not be forgotten that modernity is rejected and spurned just as many times as it is embraced.

Yet when we come to talk about poetry, modernity – the idea that a work of art consciously deals with the representation of the present and breaks with the re-iterative function of authority and tradition – cannot be overlaid exactly by what critics, tracing the history of 20th century styles, referred to as modernism. Modernity is after all the guiding figure of Romantic poetry no less than it is the touchstone of major modernists who were concerned with immediacy and process in their work; and its influence is certainly felt in the ironic absent presence behind so much post-modern criticism. Indeed one of the first things which might be said about a modern poem, thus broadly defined, is that it is a poem which in some way or other has time within it: modern poetry is a poetry which brings to the fore the question of a conscious and self conscious representation of time. This time may be the historical, biographical time of a Romantic or of a confessional poet; or it may be the relativistic process time of major American modernists like William Carlos Williams or Charles Olson. Thus, Williams's "The Red Wheelbarrow" stresses time as a sharp, sensational instance whereas Wordsworth's "The Prelude" stresses time as a type of ongoing, recollective and formative memory: but both poems are modern in that both engage with time's movement and posit the creative production of time at the core of the poetic work. As the poet and critic Octavio Paz put it, modern poetry is that poetry in which the poem

---

70 First published as "The Myth of Origins" in *Absence and Negativity, Southerly* 60, Number 2, Halstead Press, Sydney 2000

who wants to create Australia?

creates and enacts itself as an analogue to the fullness of temporal experience.[71] The modern poem re-enacts time. And in re-enacting time, it enacts a position which the individual takes up within that time – confessionally, symbolically, structurally.

Modernity, however, is also a discourse to do with evacuation, emptiness and removal. This contrary theme is no less powerful than the theme do with the enactment of 'full' experience. These two opposing themes seem to require each other (somewhat like yin and yang) in that the very desire to place poem and self in time cannot but open up a contrary reflection upon language, upon words, upon the temporal medium that poets use. Words look too provisional, too material and too inadequate for a the task of capturing a full, time-filled moment of experience. This contrary theme, in short is the theme of "silence" – a theme which extends from Wordsworth's image of thoughts too deep for words (an inexpressible, an unconscious, an immanence) through to what a contemporary critic like Ihab Hassan identifies as a core element of 20th century modernist writing – the presence of a "negative, acting through art, language, and consciousness".[72] The modern poem may intend to be an immanent representation of time, but the very language in which poetry is written underscores a negativity in poetry whose words are meaningless, precarious, empty.

Hassan's brief genealogy of modern "silence" is worth considering here in more detail. First, he writes:

> Romantic dream and metaphor explode words into outrageous visions.
> Second, Romantic irony, taking a parallel line through Heine and
> Mallarmé, moves the imagination towards its abolition, and persuades art
> of its own impossibility...[73]

Irony, the deeply ironic placement of language in time, persuades poetry of its own silence. Its time-filled, momentary voice sings to the nightingale as a prelude to loss, to death, to a recognition that the word "forlorn" is *both* expressive of a real state of mind *and* no more than a term, a mere word (the "very word") which recalls Keats to his "sole self". A mere word, that is, a mere self: or, rather, the fact that thought and feeling are merely transient words. At its simplest level, modernity in poetry is that feature which constantly undermines the truth of fervent, expressive language with the reminder that the words are representations and empty signs. All such wakeful, rational designs of the poet seeking to re-enact experience are tied to the inexpressible, to the moment out of mind, to the recognition that poetry is artifice, that utterance is an empty shell.

This contradictory theme is a theme everywhere manifested in Romantic and modernist writing: it is, it might be suggested, *the* predicament of modernity. Each expression, each isolated imagist instance, each sensation symbolically transacted in the poem, each framing of the moment or the experience, is empty language. It is voice not only addressing the void, but itself composing the void. If in the philosopher Giorgio Agamben's succinct phrase, commenting on the history of Western poetics, "thinking death is simply thinking The Voice"[74] then some such contradictory or

---

71 Octavio Paz, *Children of the Mire: Modern Poetry from Romanticism to the Avant-Garde*, trans Rachel Phillips, Harvard University Press, Cambridge, Mass., 1974, p 58ff

72 Ihab Hassan, *The Dismemberment of Orpheus: Towards a Post-Modern Literature*, Oxford University Press, New York 1971, p 14

73 Hassan, op cit, p 7

74 Giorgio Agamben, *Language and Death: The Place of Negativity*, trans Karen E Pinkus, University of Minnesota Press, Minnesota, 1991, p 60

modernity: five fragments **69**

dialectical "vision" of modernity is held by every major poet or critic who responds to the profound ontological rift which the notion of the modern opens up. It is a theme which is continuous from Wordsworth's memory of himself suddenly alone, suddenly halting as he skates across the frozen lake and finding himself in an empty spinning cosmos right through to the interfacing "skating" surfaces of John Ashbery's poem "The Skaters". Both are modern poems; both are analogues in Paz's sense in that they are poems which attempt to recreate the space and time of an experience. Both are flickering with the weight of the empty/full moment. For at the heart of analogy, says Paz, lies emptiness. [75] And again, commenting specifically on the work of Mallarmé, "The nothingness which is the world turns itself into a book: the Book...but the book does not exist; it was never written. Analogy ends in silence."[76]

a banyan tree

The banyan tree (*ficus religiosa*) is somewhat like the Moreton Bay fig: like the Moreton Bay, the banyan produces aerial roots which grow down to the ground and which ultimately become secondary trunks for the tree's wide-spreading branches. It is, so to speak, a many-rooted tree and, as such, provides a genealogical image for production and inheritance somewhat more complex than the usual single-stemmed tree with which we are familiar in those Hegelian and Darwinian accounts of the branching of cultures or of the splitting of genera into species. True, the interplay of biological and botanical metaphors of this sort is complex; but it is fairly safe to say that the ramifying tree still provides a powerful residual image for the dissemination (seeding) of cultures, ideas, literary styles. The Darwinian form of this tree, for instance, offers the form in which people talk about how a culture grows up, growing more diverse as it does so; likewise, the same single-stemmed tree image is often at work in those accounts of colonial culture which talk of Australian culture as an off-shoot or which talk of the transplanting of an idea from one place to another. In all such accounts, an assumption is made that culture is like the single, old tree, renewing its growth and growing from a single centre. The banyan, however, significantly modifies a unifying approach. In the banyan, new roots can be grown and new outgrowths form trunks from *any* point along the branch. The banyan does not have a single stem.

This multi-stemmed facet of the banyan made it a useful image for the literary historiographer and critic H.M.Green. Green, obviously uncomfortable with simplistic notions of "offshoot", "outgrowth" and "transplant", employed the image of the banyan in the preface to his *A History of Australian Literature: Pure and Applied* when he wanted to find a way to position Australian writing within the canopy of English literature and of other literatures in English. "This great literature," he writes, "is like a banyan-tree, whose branches bend down, and striking the ground, take root and grow up as independent individuals."[77] Australian literature, in short, is not simply a Darwinian offshoot, but the creative result of an overarching canopy reaching down to Australian earth whose branchwork is still (as in the banyan) integral to the main tree.

75 Octavio Paz, *Children of the Mire*, op cit, p 71

76 Paz, op cit, p 77

77 H.M. Green, *A History of Australian Literature: Pure and Applied*, Vol 1 1789–1923, Angus and Robertson, 1961, p xi

Ultimately, we must suppose, a parallel tradition will occur, a new tradition which like the banyan's many trunks is just one among many and which cannot be seen as a mere derivative or secondary branch.

The banyan tree image is of course still a genetic or genealogical image, no matter how much Green wants to modify it. It is an image of cultural movement still very much shaped by the idea of inheritance and natural descent. It is not in any adequate sense what a critic like Edward Said would call an image of an affiliative relationship to culture and aesthetics; which is to say, it is not an image to do with cultural connections which accrue around pieces of writing or to do with addressing the linkages which the texts themselves construct with what is "other" and often extraneous to the inherited tradition.[78] The banyan is a vertical image of descent rather and not a horizontal image derived from travel, the crossing of frontiers and exchange.

The study of Australian poetry is formed almost entirely according to an underlying genetic model. Emergence, influence, inheritance, generational representativeness, the influence of political and biographical context work as largely unchallenged concepts underpinning a local poetics. Like the grain seen lengthways down a piece of wood, the alignment of these traditional literary classifications (together with their metaphoric power) is almost invariably linear: inheritances stretch backward to single points and places in time, fulfilment is treated like a pre-determined flowering.

Unlike the affiliative and lateralising view, genetic accounts are narrow, familial versions of literary history, much preoccupied with influences and derivations. They are often fed by the fact that much literary criticism in Australia is a form of philology or literary history or literary biography: very often this work is rapidly translated into interpretative school readers or scholarly companions, locking generations of potential future readers into the latest and usually simplifying genetic account. Each new literary generation "fills in" the latest space, adding its voice to whatever version of the ramifying tree is on offer at the time. So, to take a recent instance: an essay entry in a companion argues (admittedly, for the complex and interesting reason that a generational definition simply does not fit the work) the necessity to invent a new "generation" to explain what has happened in recent poetry publishing.[79] Genetics tends to reach for this sort of single-level "explanation" and in so doing not only narrows the possible field of connections in which poetry can be seen to operate but also risks enforcing (in the minds of the writers themselves) a permanently blind kind of contemporariness. This is the contemporariness which knows only that each new generation is the latest generation and which leads to what I would call an endlessly repeated moment of contemporary overthrow by which each of these new, self-defined generations feels it must start from scratch, that what has gone before is irrelevant, often indeed that there is no significant contextual poetics in the local scene.

A brief example of the over-emphatic and distorting effects of genetic reading is to be found, for example, in the following, important claims made by the poet John

---

78 Edward W. Said, *The World, the Text and the Critic*, Faber and Faber, London, 1984, p 19. "What I am describing is the transition from a failed idea or possibility of filiation to a kind of compensatory order that, whether it is a party, an institution, a set of beliefs, or even a world-vision, provides men and women with a new form of relationship, which I have been callling affiliation but which is also a new system." And p 175 passim: "To recreate the affiliative network is... to make visible, to give materiality back to, the strands holding the text to society, author and culture."
79 David McCooey, "Contemporary Poetry: Across Party Lines" in ed Elizabeth Webby, *The Cambridge Companion to Australian Literature*, Cambridge University Press, Cambridge, UK 2000 p 158ff

Tranter when introducing a selection of the so-called "new" Australian poets back in 1979:

> (h)owever diverse these poets are, a general aim can be seen in the development of their work over the last ten years, and it can most usefully be seen in terms of the modernist movement. As either blindness or hostility to the importance of this tradition is a part of Australia's cultural insularity, it might be worthwhile to outline some of (modernism's) implications briefly here [80]

All well and good, no doubt, as a way of portraying an intention, a feel for what one was doing. As has been much commented on, there was a strong feeling at the time that many aspects of modernist poetry had not been reckoned with by Australian poets, particularly experimental and urban ways of writing. But looking back, it has to be asked in what sense could an overview of "Australia's cultural insularity" which took in earlier writers as diverse as Brennan, Wright, Slessor, Campbell or Webb be seen as evidence of a hostility or blindness towards modernism? How insular was or is a country which produced such writers? If there was certainly anti-modernism in the air, were these writers anti-modernist? Outside a narrowly genealogical view (in this family tree, the children's genetic drive was presumably to have done with the influence of the parents) the poets just mentioned all express significant, practical connections with major themes of modernist poetry. Arguably their work constitutes a central modernist moment in Australian poetry. One is a proto-modernist symbolist, one is a major poet of relativity, ecology and Einsteinian physics, one writes the greatest Australian poem about intermediate mind-state and the relativistic nature of temporal experience, one is the lyric poet of cubism and second generation Spanish *modernismo*, and the last is one of the great poets of the psychiatric condition and inner exploration.

Back in 1979, none of this provided a powerful enough local experience of modern and modernist writing. None of it offered an insight into modernity. A locally modern poetic context was invisible to a generation searching genealogically for its own distinctive stylistic ancestry. As is now well known, that ancestry was invented in, virtually adopted from, the work of a previous, already established group of late modernist American poets, for the most part the New York school. As a result the modernity of local Australian writers was obscured: they simply did not represent the right kind of late modernism. There seemed to be no point of origin to go back to in which a spark of modernity could be identified. Instead there was a lack of connection, a lack which relates to the pervasive, reiterated sense that (in both poetry and criticism) Australian poetry as a whole lacks a point of origin and that the ramifying image of the banyan is simply not strong enough to constitute a foundation. "Australian poets," as Paul Kane puts it, "have been forced to come to terms with that gap or negativity in their poetic heritage in order to establish an origin for their own poetry".[81] This absence, this inability to find a name for the authenticating x-factor which legitimates the ancestry of a local strand of poetry, whether that point of origin is a dreamt about tradition of modernist renewal or the work of a 19th century visionary poet like Whitman, is so often repeated that according to Kane, "this recurrent process

---

80 John Tranter ed., *The New Australian Poetry*, Makar Press, St Lucia, 1979, p xviii

81 Paul Kane, *Australian Poetry: Romanticism and Negativity*, Cambridge University Press, Cambridge, 1996, p 51

[of coming to terms with the absence of an originating figure] becomes the history of Australian poetry".[82]

a language of origins

A few years ago, I came across an article which reprinted some very early poems of Sylvia Plath. The poems were juvenilia, work written in high school. They made a lasting impression on me, not least because they were striking and energetic pieces.

Two other features were immediately remarkable about them – firstly, that they bore few if any anticipative signs of the poetry for which Plath is now well known. Many were often declarative, slightly rhetorical and neo-formal poems, largely lacking the intensity and word play which became Plath's hall mark. Many show the submerged influences of Auden. Others were written in an open, variable measure; they were even slightly jazzy in their talkative, pointed way.[83] They were, in a certain sense, quintessentially 1950-ish modern American poems, less stiff than their British counterparts; at their best, they combined a talkative prosaic mode with a confident sense of rhythmic organisation. If written today (rather than by a teenager and university student in the 1950s) they would still be sufficiently accomplished, by the standards of any creative approach to the teaching of writing, to hold their own as poems. This is perhaps why Ted Hughes published a selection of them as "Juvenilia" in the back of his edition of Plath's *Collected Poems*. But again, they certainly are not true "Plath". They are written in what I would call the residual, available manner and diction of poetry; they represent what an equally intelligent reader or writer, living at the time, could assume to be poetry. Ultimately, though well written, they are not independent enough to be read as more than an appendix or an introduction to Plath's later work. The reason for this, which is both the strength and the limitation of these juvenilia, is because their ease is sub-poetic. They are too available, too readily attuned, to what the common ear and expectation of poetry was in the 1950s.

Reading these pieces of Plath's started me thinking about what such residual sub-poetries are in different places and different times. For one thing, they are not languages which lack expertness. They are not poetry at the level of doggerel; they are poems which over-represent a feeling for poetry as a memorable form of artifice. They over-represent the artifice which the general (and much of the critical) community can accept. These sub-poetries are what we remember poetry to be; they reflect the manner in which we expect our local ear to be attuned to verse and they are different within differing communities and traditions. Plath's talkative, jazzy poems came from the zone of that acceptable artifice, no less than a British poet might have to change and develop the expectation that the long tradition of variations on blank verse and the quatrain form a deep, residual expectation in the mind of any British reader as to what a poem shall be. No less perhaps than a poet writing in French might have to deal with the peculiar admixture of intensely lyrical phrasing and prosaic form which modern French readers identify as the form of the poem. These residual sub-poetries are, in short, part of what the 19th century symbolist poet Mallarmé termed as the language

---

82 Ibid
83 I am thinking of poems like "April 18th", "Gold Mouths Cry," "Aerialist," "Morning in the Hospital Solarium" which are collected in *Sylvia Plath: Collected Poems*, ed. Ted Hughes, Faber and Faber, London,1981

of the tribe: they are the language in which poetic memory first forms itself when unalloyed with the self conscious demands of modernity.

And here? We are insistently told that ballad form and bush poetry constitute that residual, memorable form. It may be true to a certain extent. It is often the case that a resort to simply-phrased, mainly rhyming poetry is not uncommon because these traditional formal elements offer an acceptable public format for the poem. Popular poetries like theatre-sports contest poems, poems performed in the poetry competition in Bourke, an ABC broadcast of a poem specially composed by the mates of a local policeman and recited at his funeral after a night-club shooting: these instances spring to mind as recent moments where a slangy, rhyming verse form has been utilised for acceptable public sentiment. But in my experience the residual, memorable poetry of this country is not quite of this kind, at least not deeply so. These semi-doggerel poems are public, whereas the vast majority of the poems encountered in reading for magazines or brought in by students to classes (or, no doubt, written by countless Australians and shown to no-one) are less concerned with demonstrating public response and more addressed to central matters of self and place. They are often directly to do with subjective feelings in relation to landscape and time. In the main, they are in loose, non-rhymed stanzas; they take minor instances of ordinary experience as their focus, and their tone is mostly downbeat, self-admonishing and transient. They are poems of environment and local residence. They are poems in which the writers search for correspondences between emotion and space. Not surprisingly (and this can be depressing) they have that same transparency of diction which Plath's juvenile poetry has: in other words, they often lack consciously colloquial or vernacular phrasing and they lack the tense contours which specific, individual pressures make on a poet's language.

Significant poetry, the work of poets, never loses a relationship with the residual sub-poetry of the period in which it is written. Good poetry is a transformation of this residual style of ingrained poetic memory. If a proper place for the origin of poetry had to be found, then it would be in this relationship between significant poetry and these memorable sub-poetries. Clearly, I am suggesting that the sub-poetry of Australians is identified in a loosely symbolist, in many respects early or proto-modernist poetry of reminiscence and topography. Its poetic figure is mostly that of real or imaginary landscape.

eroded hills

For Octavio Paz, the crucible of modernity is the paradox of time and appearance: this paradox is to do with how linguistic expression is both true and an empty representation at the same time. That is why for him poetry can be both "pure time" and a "heartbeat of presence in the moment of its appearance/disappearance".[84] Poetry deals with both full and empty representations of things, calibrating the meanings of both values, measuring both the empty and the full. A poem is not just to do with how things are, but whether they are; and in that sense all poetry has an ontological reference. Adopting George Steiner's phrase, we could see this aspect of modern poetry as part of the much deeper "ontological" difficulty which he identifies in modern and in

---

84 Octavio Paz, *Children of the Mire*, op cit, p 164

particular post-war poetry. This ontological difficulty results from the way in which (to borrow the famous critic's terms) many poems put in question the "existential suppositions" behind poetry which guarantee that poems make sense, refer to the real or engage with human speech in a straightforward way.[85] Steiner reserves this term mainly for poetry which specifically breaks the communicative contract between poet and reader – for poems, in short, which do not "make sense" – and he locates ontological difficulty as primarily an aspect of language and naming.

Yet the difficulty Steiner identifies is much more widespread than only those poems (such as Celan's, for instance) which radicalise the practice of naming. Modern poetry commonly poses questions about the ontological status of what is presented, troubling the nature of meaning and negotiating between a zone of non-being (intention, expectation, future sense, perception, response) and a zone of being (things, meanings, events, histories.) The short, famous poem mentioned earlier, William Carlos Williams's "The Red Wheelbarrow," is a poem of this sort, making, as it says, so much "depend" on the wheelbarrow, making, that is, so much depend on its being there. Modern poetry in general stresses how the imaginative act – particularly, what Wallace Stevens called "the poem of the act of the mind" – can bring things into existence, measuring the degree to which language allows what it references to "be" there or "not be" there.[86] Poets like Baudelaire, Mallarmé and Paz, for instance, see this relation between poetry and reality as a matter of "correspondence" or analogue; in short, they see it as a matter of a necessary rhythmic and imaginative congruence between poem as artifact (empty representation) and the fullness of the world. Correspondence could be, as in Mallarmé's case, an audible music carried in the structure of the line and in the voicing of the poem or it could be in the form of an "inner" music of image and narrative; or it could be a calibration, an attunement, between the subjective experience and objective event. T.S. Eliot reformulated this latter sense of correspondence more specifically in terms of the poetic image when he coined his famous phrase "objective correlative", a term he uses to describe an image which is not reducible to a single meaning or a single feeling but which intuitively and liminally carries the narrative weight of a sensation and thought.

Paz's crucible of modernity fired the minds of mid-20th century Australian poets no less than it did Latin American writers. "Eroded Hills," for example, is a short and widely anthologised poem by Judith Wright, first collected in her 1953 volume, *The Gateway*.[87] The figure traced in this and similar poems is a figure thinkable only within the context of modernity: it is the figure of time passing, of the poem holding that moment in a phase of appearance and disappearance, and of the poet's own reckoning with the fragility and non-reality of "state of mind" issues connected with this moment of perception. It is a figure repeated again and again throughout the work of Australian poets:

> These hills my father's father stripped,
> and beggars to the winter wind
> they crouch like shoulders naked and whipped -
> humble, abandoned, out of mind.

85 George Steiner, *On Difficulty and Other Essays*, Oxford University Press, New York, 1978, p 40 passim

86 Wallace Stevens, *Of Modern Poetry*, Alfred A. Knopf, New York, 1981, p 239

87 Judith Wright, *Collected Poems 1942–1970*, Angus and Robertson, Sydney,1971, p 83

Of their scant creeks I drank once
and ate sour cherries from old trees
found in their gullies fruiting by chance.
Neither fruit nor water gave my mind ease.

I dream of hills bandaged in snow,
their eyelids clenched to keep out fear.
When the last leaf and bird go
let my thoughts stand like trees here.

Of course we can read this poem genealogically too, tracing, for instance, the obvious influence of Shakespeare and Yeats on its phrasing and prosody. We can read it too under another genealogical paradigm to do with the colonial and post-colonial perceptions of cleared land. The ominous line "When the last leaf and bird go" certainly suggests an anticipated barrenness and sterility easily associated with ecological mismanagement. Yet the poem is centrally to do with the transposition of a state-of-mind consideration on to a vision of eroded hills; it is about correspondence, and arguably about non-correspondence. At its heart is an ontological difficulty common both to modernist and symbolist poetry, a difficulty expressed in the invocation "let my thoughts stand like trees". We know that Wright's thoughts will *not* stand there like real trees; we know that the reference to trees is an image only of what will perhaps stand through time: her thoughts and intentions. We know, as it were, that it is just an image, just language. The interplay of Paz's appearance/disappearance is consummately handled in "Eroded Hills". When the purely cultural and literary historical perspectives, whether of ecology or antipodeanism, with which we read a poem like "Eroded Hills" have faded from view the poem will continue to perform its acts of appearance/disappearance.

The same is true of much of the work of a contemporary of Wright's, David Campbell. In a poem such as "Menindee", for example, there is even a pronounced sense of a modern and flatter painterly space in which events are clustered rather than positioned narratively in a traditional form of perspective: [88]

Long-sighted aloof the explorers
Set out last century
The town waits in the bend of the river
An outpost a depot
Seasons and tourists cross the plains
Melt into the mirage water
A red kangaroo with frail forepaws
Stands like a monument
Like the front sight of a rifle –
A clutch of inked-in emus
Last year's chicks
Long-legged as schoolgirls
And as curious
Gathers if you wave a handkerchief
And laughing three aboriginals
Enter the public bar
Of Maiden's Hotel Est. 1856

---

88 David Campbell, *The Man In the Honeysuckle*, Angus and Robertson, Sydney, 1979, p 51

Campbell's poetry as a whole is often overtly taken up with the themes of relativist cosmology and deeply influenced by mainstream modernist picture space, including that of Aboriginal carving and painting. In this deceptively simple poem, a single temporal relationship with historical events is displaced into several different times which only the poem can compose. Again the poem stresses its paradoxical ontological bearing on the events it describes. Its images capture a seemingly timeless state of mind, whilst all the while stressing movement, congregation, community. Writing (the representative means of poetic language, the brief clarity of voicing) is at odds with the placement of the huge empty space of inland New South Wales around Menindee; yet, despite that sense of empty spaciousness, the poem forms a completely adequate symbolic moment of perception in time and place. It cannot be stressed enough how powerfully these themes are felt not just in Campbell but across a range of work from Brennan through to Murray: among them are the key modern themes of the problematic nature of transcendence, the problem of the something and the nothing, no less than the themes associated with a relativity of position in the observer's experience in space and time. Indeed, a key critical challenge would be to find, among the more important poets, the ones who do *not* have this relationship with the ontological difficulties of self and placement.

"Silva", Robert Adamson's poem, published in the late 80s nearly a decade after Campbell's "Menindee", directly addresses the ontological theme of placement.[89] Significantly, Adamson deals here with many of the central themes of modernity including conflictive themes in the nature of modern experience and a deep sense of contradiction in the nature of the "old languages" referred to in the poem. This is a writing which is much more densely informatic, with its images forming a flow or a flood of shifting meanings. Further, the placid voicing of the poem as an unambiguously European voice has been disrupted. Who are we? its voice seems to be asking. What is it which has come into being? No less than in Wright and Campbell, the absence expressed in the poem is an absence of attachment and an absence of identification between the two contemporary histories, one of European settlement and the other of Aboriginal presence, which have occurred side by side in modern Australia:

It came into being from the splintered limbs
swam out and flowered into being

from chopped saplings and wood-chips
its pages glowing and telling their numbers

this a numbat's fragile skeleton
this the imprint of the last chalk-moth

Members of court in the old languages
mumbled as wings of ground parrots flicked

At night we discovered new seeds
in an old gum's stump as shoals of insect memory

floated out from a bee-eater's nest
then the rasping call of an adder

We looked into the white-rimmed eyes of the elders
and wanted to turn away

89 Robert Adamson, *Mulberry Leaves: New and Selected Poems 1970–2001*, Paper Bark Press, Sydney 2001, p 180

until pages began stroking air
that carried back doves from the black bamboo
Australia the goshawk circled a lake
we croaked amphibian prayers to reflected skies

then stumbled off through the spinifex

Mornings threaded the whale bones with flame
as poetry baked like a rock

on the final page of dense black marble
of slate-thought that shone

until the eyes of a huntsman took us
into morning's spokes a white trap-work

where caught finches hung their hearts drumming

Australia we sobbed through the paperbarks' songs
to birds and the gentle animals

and to the soft-stepping people of its river-banks

All three poems amplify the theme of psychological correspondence: none more than Adamson's with its haunting and ambivalent sense of who "we" are and its sense of an interpenetration between the "place" of the living and the "place" of the dead, of those present and of those dispossessed. These poems operate in the heartland of the empty/full moment which Paz so well defines. But they are modern in another closely related sense, too. An awareness of the limits of language and experience, based in an experience of absence or loss, responds in an up-to-date way to the matters of dislocation, killing, settlement and traditional custodianship which are so much a part of a cross-cultural sense of Australia. Such a concern is overtly evidenced in Adamson's poem with its references to the "white-rimmed eyes of the elders" and to the "soft-stepping" riverside people; but it is true also when we re-consider the timeless shifting perspectives of historical time in Campbell's poem or probe the reasons for the erosion and tree clearance in Judith Wright's poem. The beggars crouching like "shoulders naked and whipped" quickly lose their lyrical landscapist reference. These poems have, in this regard, neither ancestry nor no ancestry; they suffer not so much from a generalised literary historical negativity than the negativity each poem itself proposes. They are open to the absences which they relate, open to another possible fullness. Such poems key into matters which, still under-acknowledged, are at the core of Australian poetics.

going on

Thinking critically about poetry will always turn out to be inconclusive, perhaps to the chagrin of the theorist. Sensitised and intuitive, critical writing is at best a contribution to collective responses to art. Criticism itself, however, cannot help but deal with philosophical categories to do with perception and language. Arguably, if there is a lack in Australian criticism at present, then it is probably a lack related to this latter area of responsiveness: critical terms adequate, fresh enough, to describe the insights and objective perceptions in the work of the poets have not been invented locally. Classifying systems, largely derived from English and American critics and historians, are applied to Australian writing, as if genetic accounts and histories of evolution similar to those of British and American writing can be mapped equidistantly across the structures of connection, response and contact which form the local histories of a local art. Borrowed terms like "pastoral", "urban" and "landscape", for instance, may work very differently or simply may not work at all when applied to Australian poetry.

Likewise, the fact that the mainstream of Australian poetry is a poetry based in the heart of issues to do with modernity is rarely evinced satisfactorily. Genetic matters, aerial or ramifying systems, disguise the need to look at re-iterative figures in our poetry. But to look at these figures, to see the way in which Australian poetics is obsessed with placement, with writability, with ontological difficulty, may be one way of shifting the burden of absence which can indeed be identified in our modern 20th century tradition. The very attempt to find a previous "El Dorado" of originary philosophical achievement (that is to say, to find a moment of founding intellectual genius equivalent to the impact of Emerson and Whitman on American poetics or Hegel, Goethe and Schiller on German) runs the risk that one overlooks the recurrence of other prominent features in many Australian poets' engagement with their own sense of modernity.

This engagement, I have suggested, is strongest felt in that aspect of Australian poetry where there is also a conscious reflection on the part of the poets about the relationship between a significant poem and what was earlier termed the poetry of common memory and expectation. It is felt too in a recurrent image of location and dislocation and a need to address the matter of ancestry on a trajectory which includes but is broader than literary inheritance alone. To bring two or three poems, "Eroded Hills", "Menindee" and "Silva", to critical attention is most likely a gesture no more important than to spin a few, finely shaped pebbles out across a lake. But if something comes through of a way to rethink the way critics classify thematic relationships and deal with historical influences and perhaps too if something comes through of the need for a philosophical realigning of some critical terms normally adopted when talking about Australian poets, then the hope would be that the dislodgement of those few pebbles is sufficient to start at least a few new waves.

digitalism

"I felt justified in experimenting" – Blackout

Two poem-sequences have appeared recently which reflect aspects of the digital nature of contemporary writing systems and take other pieces of writing as substantial starting points for the new work. M.T.C. Cronin's "Talking with Neruda's Questions" and John Tranter's "Blackout",[90] could loosely be described as cut-ups or samples of well-known or at least significant pieces of previous literature. The first takes as its ur-text the great Chilean modernist poet Pablo Neruda's final and posthumously published sequence, *A Book of Questions*; the second takes an even more canonised and critically important text, Shakespeare's *The Tempest*, using it as a maquette or boiler plate for a cut-up text.

Strikingly, neither of the contemporary poems handles this connection with a "classical" original poem in a traditional literary manner. M.T.C. Cronin's "Talking with Neruda's Questions" openly foregrounds the experimental nature of the contemporary poem's connection with the famous older work. Thus, contrary to the idea that her poem might be a homage to an influential dead poet Neruda's presence is largely erased. The relationship between the new poem and the older one involves less personal translation than extensive textual interchange. As if to stress the textual arbitrariness of her view of the original poem Cronin makes use of an already published translation, William O'Daly's 1991 version.[91] The poet deliberately lets us know that her version takes off from a text which is not, *stricto sensu*, the original Spanish language poem.

A similar idea that the literary source behind a new poem is provisional is also a feature of "Blackout." Tranter mixes up samples of an ancient text with samples from two other modern texts. More, neither of these secondary texts is a poem.[92] What results is accordingly an ongoing and perhaps deliberately incomplete work in which digitally processed interweavings and cancellations between the three pieces of writing lead on to the currently published poem. Connections which are properly assumed to operate between a famous literary example and a new poem are deliberately taken

---

90 M.T.C. Cronin, *Talking with Neruda's Questions*, Vagabond Press, Sydney 2001; John Tranter, *Blackout*, Vagabond Press, Sydney 2000. An earlier version of some of the comments made here appeared in a review in *Australian Book Review*, October 2000 and in a postface note to M.T.C. Cronin's *Talking with Neruda's Questions*

91 See Pablo Neruda: *The Book of Questions/El libro de las preguntas* trans William O'Daly, Copper Canyon Press, Port Townsend, Washington, 1991

92 John Tranter lists the other two pieces as an article by Joan Didion and a chapter from Tom Wolfe's *The Electric Kool Acid Test*

apart and broken. Any attempt to argue an explicit reason for the fragmentation of the original in, say, the manner which Pound combined samples in *The Cantos* in his famous vortices of fragments is rejected in favour of a method of juxtaposition which puts together a single-level linear text where the breaks between different sources for the materials are hard to recognise. Bits and pieces of the original works flicker through Tranter's poem like bright stones in a mosaic. Some can be identified; others cannot. Their recognisability is, in the main, haphazard, leaving the reader with the impression that the processing of the materials is in large part machine made and aleatoric. The result is a poem which is curiously independent of its famous ancestor; there is almost a suggestion that any famous poem might have done the job.

What then is the criterion of selection where the original materials of these two poems are concerned? An answer will inevitably encompass a shift (a moment which could be categorised as a moment of indirection) between a digitalised sense of the literary past and a set of other traditionally established ways of acknowledging literary inheritance – such as literary forms like homage. Translation, pastiche, imitation, paraphrase could all be mentioned here too. Broadly speaking, all these forms derive from the practices of Renaissance poets and whether literal translation or literary imitation, they all imply a direct connection between the original source work and the new work. These were, for instance, the forms in which 17th and 18th Century poets reclaimed the main works of classical antiquity; they remain the means by which poets introduce foreign modes and genres into the vernacular literature. Homage and translation, in other words, are tried and true methods of an analogue, or copying, way of rendering an earlier work. The new text while not necessarily being a literal facsimile has nonetheless the status of being a version authenticated by the original. At heart, analogue methods *assume* that the new poem, no matter how transformed or even deliberately distorted, is to be judged as a reproduction of the original. Their relation to the original is similar to that of a photograph: no matter how blurred or recoloured a photograph, it is at base inevitably considered as a reproduction of an original subject. It is this necessary connection with the previous text which both "Blackout" and "Talking with Neruda's Questions" make precarious. They grow from earlier texts very clearly, but they do not reproduce them or translate them. Any notion of equivalence is left unclear.

In these poems, then, equivalence is not the main game. Factors of chance and factors of change are. *The Book of Questions*, a sequence of seventy four short poems cast in the form of questions, demonstrates this sharply. Much as if entering a different key stroke instruction, Cronin's version shifts the syntactic device from a question format to a statement format while retaining much of the language, the imagery and metaphors and keeping to the same number of seventy four short poems. What matters here is not to make a new version but to intervene in an existing text and make a deep structural change. Where necessary and where Neruda's questions do not answer themselves, new phrases are provided. Clearly, however, what is recycled from the original text is not a copy of its structural impact, nor a rendering of the dramatic voicing of Neruda's poem.

The act of sampling is, however, not undeliberated. Many of Neruda's images are used in a way which is off centre and foreign to English language norms. So we get

> The name of the month between December
> and January is Little-Month-Without-Cares.
>
> By the authority of the three-handed vintner
> they numbered the twelve grapes of the cluster...[93]

Neruda's poem is *replaced* in front of us no longer as a formal whole but in bits and pieces; while at the same time its voicing and syntax are converted into a hidden template which dictates what new material can be introduced. The result is inevitably a poem which has been dehistoricised and decontextualised. But paradoxically the new poem demonstrates how the partly surrealist influenced images of a modernist can function in the work of a contemporary Australian. Thus Cronin transposes Neruda's fifty seventh question into:

> If we outlawed interplanetary kisses
> would we need a prison-cage of moonbeams?
>
> And would a court of love
> try the kissers in their beds?
>
> The platypus in its spacesuit
> could round up the offenders
>
> and the horses in their quiet shoes
> could look for evidence on the moon.[94]

Sampling (in the musical sense, for instance) is a useful term here. Cronin's poem relocates parts of Neruda's poem. She deals not with the Spanish original literally, but with a version of it capturing fragments of Neruda's poetry in much the same way that one might scan an image or part of an image in the construction of a digital collage. The whole question of what Neruda's original means to us now, including the historical question of what the poem meant when first composed, is sidelined. Cronin's poem, for example, makes little overall narrative sense whereas Neruda's, though full of paradoxical references, structures a series of questions for a resolved formal effect. Neruda's poem, a set of questions asked by someone at the edge of death, casting an eye back on his life, is a rhetorical schema with a powerful, theatrical and persuasive meaning overall. Every reader intensely senses that the poem could only have been written at that particular point in Neruda's life at *that* moment, in *that* crisis. The formal effect is so strong that the biographical context, the poem's posthumous publication, even extra-literary facts such as the confrontational political environment Neruda was writing in seem necessarily to add to its meaningfulness. These features work so tightly as analogues to the poem's apparent textual meanings that, biographical and contextual elements though they may be, they cannot easily be extrapolated from Neruda's intentions in writing the poem. Their convergence is historical and infrangible. They are, so to speak, "in" the writing. Very tellingly, they are largely excised in Cronin's digital reuse of the poetry.

2

Unlike the finality and historicity of *The Tempest* and of *The Book of Questions*, malleability at the level of units of information is one of the hallmarks of digital systems. Such

---

93 M.T.C. Cronin op cit, unnumbered pages, Poem XLVI
94 M.T.C. Cronin, op cit, Poem LVII

malleability derives ultimately from the fact that no digital representation is a copy of the original in the analogue manner just described. Rather, what a digital image presents is a statistical threshold constituted from a multiplicity of numerical samples. A sufficient number of samples, or snapshots, makes up an image but does so only when the samples have been decoded. As is often mentioned in the literature on digital aesthetics, there is no stable surface on which a digital version is captured unlike in analogue systems. There is no tape, no paper, no photographic surface on which a replica is indued. The absence of a copy is, in every sense of the word, literal.

One result of this is that replaceability and the theoretical possibility of manifold arbitrary associations appear to be inbuilt into the logic of digital operations. The lack of a replica opens up too the possibility of selecting only some of the snapshots rather than all of them, or of modifying these snapshots in the process of capturing the information and thus significantly changing the object. This is so not only at levels which are "hidden" in the depths of the system, in its logic and programming languages. It also operates at the most surface levels of the working interface: for example, in networking, in electronic mail, in hypertext. All these structured aspects of the design system carry features of replaceability in the ways in which high speed links can be made on word or image, in the non-linear way in which information is accessed on the screen and in the non-linear design of data bases and story boards. The visual layout and design of home pages is an obvious example. Here, what typically comes up on screen is a thoroughly eclectic array of boxes and links and search engines side by side with a higgledy piggledy zoning of adverts and news links plus headers or a side image of some special display.

Neither framed picture space, neither television screen nor newspaper layout seem to explain this style of visual siting.[95] On the one hand, the average home page is a layout artist's nightmare composed of irreconcilable typefaces, print sizes, depths of field, frames and colours; but on the other hand, it displays an innovative sense of meaningfulness and composition according to which information is organised on a zoning principle which is less that of sequential reading than of reconnoitring a feature-rich space.

When these ideas are brought back to poems, a number of other features conjoins with this capacity of the digital system to produce potentially arbitrary types of corrugation in the textual surface. Perhaps the most important of these features goes to the core of the relationship between the writing of a poem and its context: the quality which was earlier described as the infrangible connection between the poem's occasion and its voicing. Digital systems loosen up that connection. Arbitrariness and a multiplicity of directions occur right from the start in any digitalised version and, indeed, reach so deeply into the purely statistical nature of structure that it becomes impossible to determine the point where and when an opening and an ending to an expression occur. Language is, so to speak, switched on rather than being commenced intentionally; and in the same manner, ending is a matter of stopping somewhat as if one is closing down the system or severing a link with the network.

If read back into the structure of poems, this seems to argue there is no necessity to build a point of resolution into the poem's narrative voice and thereby judge the right

---

95 Indeed the influence is operating the other way with some satellite TV news channels and some aspects of newspaper layout now clearly seeking to adapt the multiple and layered appearance of online screen design.

moment to terminate (exit from) the work. Similarly, when a work is reframed in digital format, it is difficult to maintain the illusion that an ending is generated from inside the writing or within inner tensions in the structure regardless of how these are carried by the fictional narrative or in the construction of the poet's voice. There is, for instance, no need to maintain the illusion that this ending coincides with a particularly privileged moment of insight or is produced through complication or Aristotelian *peripateia*. We might say that the thinking and writing which go on in a digital format no longer produce their own ends, or their own necessary time in which the outcome of a thought must be experienced. At the very least, these changes mark an important change in sensibility, arguably one already apparent in the proliferation of discontinuous forms of fiction writing, in the word-image combinations of hypertext systems and in the way that writing is more and more being treated interactively and not as static text. Analogue systems work quite otherwise: they generate a space for thought, an intensely readerly place for the voiced text, and they necessarily oblige a sense of an ending produced as part of the structure of the experience of reading. As in Neruda's poem these are features at writing's heart when practised in its analogue, representational mode.

There is a second digital characteristic which if carried over into poetry no less radically upsets the place and manner in which experience is represented. An intrinsic feature of analogue representation is that a proportion holds between original and copy. Usually this feature is a feature of miniaturisation: the image depicted in the photo, for example, is smaller than the person in real life. There are many such instances to do with images, films, paintings, books, memories, poems. Other examples are more complex because they involve intuitive and irrational types of analogue connection. Thus, the information printed on the magnetic tape is conceived as being efficiently packed into a space (the tape) much smaller than the space of the world in which the naturally occurring sound occurs. Or a child setting out toys on the carpet may have imagined the entirety of a city. Here in these examples, the impression of a miniaturisation which occurs when something is copied is clearly not just a literal analogue. For here the capacity of a version to be an analogue is metaphorically tied to a much larger phenomenological framework in which human beings perceive the relative proportions between tapes and sounds, between copies and originals, between toy cars and real ones, between pictures and their subjects. There are many such forms of half-registered identification.

Obviously, a feature such as size is not in itself the issue. In this example size indicates, rather, the way in which metaphoric proportions hold between versions and operate in a field of normal expectations about the differences of size between originals and copies. Normative relations confirm orderly sets of analogues within their phenomenological settings whilst disorderly sets disrupt those norms. This expectation of normative relationships between a thing depicted and the depiction of it can, for example, be decisive – not least in terms of emotional reaction. It is a factor which a variety of media influenced artists have recently been exploiting in work which expands the size of the object depicted either to grotesquely large proportions (Koons' installation sculptures, for instance) or to sizes which exceed the capacity of the eye to take them in. Christo's walls and fences, Smithson's land art pieces, the walking journeys of the British artist Richard Long are well known instances of an art practice which depicts terrain which is beyond the range of seeing. These works explore deliberate reversals of the normal ratio between the size of an original and its representation, a ratio which the viewer expects to operate intrinsically in analogue modalities.

But a digital version is not a replica. The intrinsically proportional relations between object and copy which an oversize Koons' artwork exploits and upsets start to weaken once it is recognised that a digital version is only a statistical sample. It is held nowhere in its entirety as a full version. The implications are complex, and should not be overstated. For instance, to draw attention to the lack of an intrinsic connection between original and replica is not to deny that the VDT's screen image is, when seen by a real viewer on a real screen, smaller or larger than the original. Obviously too a digital image may be reframed or zoomed in on or cut and resampled, thereby changing how we see it. But unlike analogue relationships these new relations between original and digital version now mainly hold according to the various forms of interface access and the variety of reuses (including size, framing, zoom) to which the stored information can be put. They no longer, first off, privilege the cause-effect connection between the original figure and the intimacy (or otherwise) of the portrayal – as in, say, the intimacy of the tiny, hand-held representation in an Elizabethan locket. Or in another example: the deliberate size of the Statue of Liberty.[96] In digital versions, expectations as to proper proportion are replaced by a willingness to reuse and recycle. You just log in the zoom instruction.

Digital systems scan, copy and reframe at will, a feature which immediately counteracts any tendency to fixate on specific attributes of the representation. Yet this breakdown of a real time affect is not about a *lack* of different attributes (colour, size, framing, focus etc.) in digital format, but quite the opposite: it is to do with how technical control of these elements analyses, breaks down and multiplies them such that they become variants which can be manipulated in any direction. What results is a new kind of precariousness in the idea that particular facets, particular features and accordingly particular responses inhere in a particular copy or are evoked by it.

This ability to frame and reframe at will is quite likely one of the reasons why John Tranter's "Blackout" is left unfinished. After the ninth section it breaks off with a printer's colophon mark indicating that there could be more words one day, or perhaps not. There could be more, there could be less. For where does such a poem start? And what kind of emotional pressures can be said to generate its language and, accordingly, what kind of pressure will bring it to an end?

3

In a chapter on the poetic use of language and the connections between imagination, writing and longing, the American poet and critic Susan Stewart writes about how emotions inhere within things and of how similarly "(w)ithout narrative, without the

---

96 An unusual but very expert example of the interplay between expectation and representation is Robert Lowell's celebrated poem, "For the Union Dead". Here Lowell uses a public Civil War statue (depicting the white Northern leader of a black "negro" regiment) in a Boston square not only as a central symbol for the theme of sacrifice but also as a comparative measure for the size and depth of historical emotion evoked by viewing TV images of the Vietnam War. Lowell and his contemporaries were watching such images (especially of body bags of killed African American soldiers) at the time and he includes them towards the end of his poem. Lowell is very consious of how different imaging systems (Civil War statues, prime time images) link in with different levels and types of response, both of numbing shock and of tragic sympathy, and evokes these differences in his magisterial anti-war poem.

organisation of experience, the event cannot come to be".[97] One claim here is that things become significant to us in so far as they deeply intertwine with emotional states like desire and longing. Further, Stewart is arguing that things (like poems, for instance) can achieve that intertwining of longing and meaning because they can *narrate* events.[98] Poetry can be exciting and emotionally engaging because it makes, as Stewart puts it, the event of the poem matter. Such a claim assumes of course that poetic language works by analogy and implies that the function of poetry is to organise specific congruencies between lived experience and the language of a poem, defining that space across a series of interlinked stories and symbolic zones. This is what was happening in Neruda's *The Book of Questions*, which is both a book of poems and a book of a "life moment". In this analogue mode, the poem brings an event into being. Largely because this identification between event and moment in speech is made so strongly in *The Book of Questions* and with such mortal seriousness, the reader is tempted to say that here the end of poetic speech symbolises the end of life, of being alive. This is the experience the poem opens up to the reader.

But "Blackout" is an "event" which is never started, never finished and about which, even more puzzlingly, it cannot even clearly be said that it is *un*finished. It does not sufficiently resolve into a coherent narrative or even a coherent thought structure for any such judgements to be certain. Nor is there a clearly established field of representation in the work. No object is nostalgised; no state of mind or place or scene is dreamt of and desired. Similarly, the polyphony of the text is left jagged and juxtapositional, much in the manner of a piece of block music. It is a downloaded text where many voices criss cross in a many timed, interactive way. Given these attributes of the poem (attributes signalled by the poem's unfinished and indeterminate nature, by its fragmentary voicing and by its lack of apparent subject matter) it is intrinsic to the work that it is hard to define what sort of an "event" "Blackout" is. It is an event entirely on the surface, taking place, so to speak, largely in its own doing.

Paradoxically then, despite all its discontinuities, "Blackout" cannot be described as self reflexive or ironically self undermining poetry. Though the poem plays with how it is artificially derived from other sources it is not a piece "about" writing: it is not about self consciously naming the terms by which the artifice of the poem's imaginary space is set up. Instead, in a way curiously opposite to a post-modernist view of poetry, "Blackout" is full of things to say, full of gestures which dramatise and commend. Indeed it is fully extroverted writing, turned away from any sense of an internal mechanism and largely ignorant of the sort of psychological "inscape" (including that of being a text about a text) which could underpin more deeply ironic manoeuvres. In a way this is another version of the discontinuous, fragmentary mode for which Tranter's poetry is often noteworthy. In an admiring, closely argued essay on Tranter, poet and novelist Alan Gould has justly observed the way his poems "are alive, often frenetic, with human exchange, and crowded with people and objects."[99] In "Blackout" the crowded, human frenzy is phrasal and syntactic. It is a mode caught in phrases like "The minute is almost done; no more passion!" or "My brain is

97 Susan Stewart, *On Longing: Narratives of the Miniature, the Gigantic, the Souvenir, the Collection*, Duke University Press, Durham and London, 1993, p 22

98 Susan Stewart, ibid

99 Alan Gould, *The Totem Ship*, Duffy and Snellgrove, Sydney, 1996, p 276

who wants to create Australia?

disturbed with my beating mind." Expressively the writing is held in a state of ongoing reframing.

Throughout, this sense of *doing*, a sense of directionality and activity in the voicing of the text, is strongly felt. Short, snappy phrases, commands, apophthegms and questions speed the language on. With no place to stop, phrases flash up and are quickly replaced. The register is dramatic, impersonal, rapid, and "textualising", inclining to make connections and to literarise. This effect is achieved more or less everywhere in the poem:

> Knife, gun, engine: prosper in the dry air,
> feed my people. No subjects govern the age.
> It is possible to live and die
> without ever meeting a Catholic or a Jew.
> Do you talk to these gentlemen?
> They always laugh at nothing.
> No-one remembers the past – then go...[100]

Linkages here are being made not only at a networked level of surface association. They seem to be coming from packets of deep memory which, in their turn, have been held in abeyance in the interlinked ur-texts from which Tranter's poem composes itself. Technically the whole poem suggests a structure closer to that of cognitive processing or of hypertext linking than that of the traditional rhetorical structures of place, evocation and description. This is writing which, not unlike neuronal encoding, is entirely in the business of making and generating, of transferring and networking. After seventeen pages, the text then breaks off.

All this is very well and very interesting. Yet one wants to and ask a question: Is there not a tortuous and possibly deceptive interplay between two contrary directions in "Blackout"? The writing seems to eschew any coherent representation of experience, including the experience of a new, turn of the millennium, Australian rendition of Shakespeare's playscript. But on the other hand, every reader ultimately stabilises Tranter's text as an extremely intense and subtle representation of a networking and associational process, including the digital and discontinuous processes just described. In short, the reader invariably makes the text into an image, even if only an image of itself. The paradox here is that, unlike an engagement with a multimedia site, the poem cannot ever quite achieve the open ended and open edged interactive format it seems to aim towards. If its readers wanted to keep the poem-text's options open in an authentically interactive way they would have to be actively writing, talking on line, exploring links or downloading as is the case, for instance, with a chatroom or computer game or other sorts of interactive site. Such reading would have to invoke, in practice, the reader as writer, the writer as reader so often celebrated in latterday critical theory.

This is not what happens. Only as an ideal, as a poetic image of reading, can "Blackout" offer a writing and a networking of a series of texts occurring in both real and virtual time. The interactive reading just described cannot take place. Instead what operates in the shift between an earlier text (Shakespeare's and others') and a later text is a moment of indirection through which a highly idealised style of reading is proposed and withdrawn. In fact the poem which we read is perhaps most properly

---

100 Tranter, op cit, p 9

described as an exploration of the limits, the unrealisability, of that moment of proposed interactivity – a withdrawal accomplished through the fact that the work inevitably returns to being "a poem" and in so far as it is a poem, to being a recreative, literary "reading space". Something similar may be said of "Talking with Neruda's Questions" where an ambiguous play between a supposedly open ended reading and the fact of a limited literary space is no less strongly felt. This is why Cronin's shifting of grammatical direction away from Neruda's dramatic question format into the form of predicate sentences is crucial. It is a manoeuvre which brings about a concertedly ambivalent effect. Whereas Neruda placed his words in resonant space, inscribing them as sharply as scratchmarks on glass, Cronin's declarative format allows for her (and Neruda's) language to be open to recycling, to recomposition and reuse. Oddly, however, at another level her reuse achieves exactly the opposite effect, locking the resonance of Neruda's language into a firmed up, structured mode like an instant digital photograph, deliberately depriving the poem's voice of quiver, dramatic pathos, imprecision and blur.

Both poems take as their material, their quarry site, poetry which expresses a deep sense of finality. Shakespeare's play is his last completed work, a work in which magical illusion is finally and definitively undone and put aside. Neruda's poem is a poem of questions at the end of a life. Deeply dramatic poems, they suggest a stopping point, a place in which poetic language ends and imagination ceases. It seems unlikely that it is just a happenstance that it is these last words and farewells which two contemporary Australian poets have adapted for their purposes. If Neruda and Shakespeare end in silence, stopping mortally, the finality of these new Australian poems is to do with the absence of analogue. It is a finality which results from all of that running about, all of that doing, all of that activity, generated in the practices of sampling and disassemblage. Their finality results from the fact that they have nothing behind them: they present or represent nothing. They do not move towards the edge, questioning it or preparing for it: they operate ceaselessly on that edge, undermining the very criteria which allow for the proper delimitation of that edge. They question whether there is an authentic threshold operating between something and nothing, illusion and reality.

Sincerity, meaningfulness, pathos, truth telling: such characteristics no longer determine the value of expressiveness in the new poems. Instead, their languages are strategies; their structures are residues of a compositional process. It is not even their abstractness which is of interest, but rather their reiterativeness, their formality, their "keeping on going" in a period when there are so many pressures to detach language from the structuring of a human intentionality. These are pressures which both these poems reflect as well as mask. Both of these pieces would speak from where we are now – which is to say, at the edge of a time of representation – but they find (inevitably, exploratively) that there is no true voice in which to do so.

what can poets teach? [101]

> *...there is a profound and irreducible antinomy between literature as practice and literature as teaching.* [102]

Reflections on a Manual is one of French critic, Roland Barthes', shortest and least known essays. Many years ago, this brief, modest essay struck me as one of the most magisterial pieces he ever wrote.

Addressed to a colloquium of secondary school literature teachers held at the Cerisy-la-Salle conference centre in 1969, *Reflections on a Manual* is an essay to do with the dullest of subjects: teaching. It is about the work of the magister (the school teacher) as he or she goes about that key activity, the transmission of knowledge. The essay portrays arguably the period's most important literary theorist and teacher reflecting on the crisis which confronted the teaching curriculum in that decade. For Barthes, that crisis reduced to three closely adjoined questions: what knowledge is now to be transmitted? And how is it to be transmitted, Barthes goes on to ask, to a generation which already appears to be becoming post-literate? Thirdly, what relevance does literature have to a generation which no longer acquires a love of literature through childhood reading?

Such questions were bold enough in their day and remain so in ours. In these few pages, Barthes succinctly lays out an ambitious programme which will address that crisis, particularly in regard to the critical teaching of literature. He presents the case for a major rethinking of how a contemporary teaching relates to classical and Romantic accounts of what is literature – a rethinking of the concepts of literature, of reading and of writing in the context of the younger generation.

The 1969 date is significant. Across Europe, it was an epoch of great change in thinking about culture, about writing, about the status of curriculum and about the received concept of literature. It is this last matter, to do with defining literature and the classical curriculum it is based on, which Barthes is mainly concerned with. Barthes goes on to say that fundamental to the received concept of literature is the way it is experienced in childhood, particularly the experience of reading the canon of great authors. Addressing the seminar at Cerisy-la-Salle a year after the so-called "May events" Barthes was concerned to anchor this received notion of literature within

---

101 A version of this essay was published in the Australian Association of Wrting Programs' on-line magazine *Text*, Volume 3, No 1, April 1999

102 Roland Barthes, *The Rustle of Language*, trans Richard Howard, Hill and Wang, New York, 1986, p 27

the whirlwind of cultural change occurring in Europe. In fact throughout the essay there are hints that he was worried his audience might be hostile, most likely because he feared that his comments would be seen as insufficiently political and would be pushed aside for ideological reasons. At various points, Barthes feels obliged to apologise for the way that his "simplistic observations"(his words) may lack applicability to the work of the literature teachers he is speaking to.

This tentativeness in no sense gainsays the fullness of the proposals he made to the colloquium on that day. The first of his three concluding proposals immediately addresses what we would now term the issue of "relevance". We should abandon, Barthes contended, all pseudo-genetic accounts of literature which allow us to "do" literary history *backwards* (his phrase). We should give over, in short, all those types of historicising description of literature which produce the present generation from the waves of previous movements, previous authors and accumulated literary influences. He proposes instead something which the intervening thirty-five years have made very familiar: the idea of teaching literature from our own interests, teaching it as a cultural object cut through with contemporary ideas and codes. Here, Barthes is both symptomatic of, and ahead of, his times, especially in the way he contends that literature can no longer be taught as an authoritative inheritance which must be rehearsed by students period by period, culture by culture, historical genre by historical genre. We should teach literature, Barthes says, with *ourselves* at the centre of its history. In teaching literature (including ancient and classical literature) literary works should become parts of an exemplary system, accessed through sign-systems, through thematic areas, through structural devices. We should read it in a way which is compatible with the reading of any other sign-system – the TV for example, or popular cultural products or a film.

***

The second proposal made by Barthes for a revision in the idea of teaching literature also constitutes a major break with tradition.

This proposal concerns his wish to "substitute *text* for author, school and movement." (Barthes' italics.) Text is here understood (in fact, significantly re-defined) as simply "a space": it is, he expands a few words further on, a site for "an infinite number of digressions". "Text" in short transcends any notion of author or of the individual purpose or the individual history of a particular piece of writing, including factual details as to how it is situated in its epoch or whether it is associated with a specific movement. Similarly, the reading of a "text" no longer necessarily utilises the trained critical elucidation of the author's intentions in the way that traditional critics put a specific priority on them or interpret meanings using the author's pre-occupations, biography or historical context as a guide. Barthes' contention back then was that a broader, generic notion of text – text-as-writing – must replace older critical classifications to do with epoch, genre, style, intention and the context of particular and previous literary influences.

The final page of *Reflections on a Manual* offers, for instance, a prophetic description of the change taking place in the practice of literature teaching, a shift which would occur through the 70s and 80s and which has put less and less emphasis on treating the text as an object specially set aside for explication, interpretation and commentary. A "sacred object" is how Barthes somewhat disparagingly styles this classically

who wants to create Australia?

conceived text: this is the text which is, in his phrase, only an "object of philology".[103] His proposal for a more updated contemporary practice locates what became for a decade or so a controversial rethinking of the terms "text" and "textuality." Text became a broad category no longer limited to a specific document and no longer modelled on, or ideally referenced by, textual objects such as an author's holograph or a specific edition. Text here – this idea is argued much more fully in other of his books like *S/Z* and in a variety of essays – defines not just the locus of interwoven themes in any piece of writing but also all the other writing and reading which become indispensably associated with any specific piece of writing.

Unlike the approach approved in the standard secondary school teaching manuals of the 60s, reading and writing are no longer to be conceived as impersonal, meditative activities devoted to revered philological objects. Reading accordingly loses something of its status, surrendering part of its function as act of interpretation and responsibility towards unknown creative work, particularly creative work of the past.

This of course is exactly where Barthes' reference to childhood and the decline in the childhood experience of literature becomes indispensable. The meditative reader, perched in the window-seat, is that young childhood reader. This is the reader who reads recreatively in isolation; this is the reader who takes away the whole bound book and reads it in its entirety, reading it as a unity of thought, language and idea. But the readers whose problems Barthes wants to address is no longer a child. With depressing accuracy Barthes sums up what remains of that practice of childhood reading for most adults in adult life: in his inventory of what "abides" from the childhood memory of reading, he lists:

> crossword puzzles, some televised quizz shows, the posters of the centenaries of some writer's birth, some writer's death, a few paperback titles, some critical illusions in the newspaper we are reading for altogether different reasons.[104]

Against this dead end of quasi-reading, the reader whom Barthes wants to bring into existence is more like a worker, or an activator, for whom reading and writing combine into an activity whose subject matter is not necessarily "literature". Instead reading and writing are, Barthes argues, productive acts, engaged across and interlinked with a plurality of texts. To study texts, to engage in this form of textualisation, is to participate in a non-hierarchical cross-reading of different sorts of text (poems, advertisements, scripts, novels, pop songs, record covers, newspaper articles, TV series and so on). When we remember that Barthes is writing this before websites, e-mail, hypertext and the array of literary and visual "readings and writings" which are part of our current electronic experience of text, the originality of his proposal is the more striking.

These thoughts were confrontational and controversial. Epoch, influence, literary genre, biographical and historical emergence, interpretative categories narrowly defined in relation to selected books and poems – all these were the stock-in-trade terms of literary history at the time. Barthes' provocative formulation that reading – a means of encoding and decoding – is what produces the entity we call text and that this level of text-making operates across all media was still scarcely entertained. Besides did

---

103 Roland Barthes, op cit, p 28
104 Roland Barthes, op cit, p 22

anyone take films and TV that seriously? Crucially Barthes sensed that it was alternative and often non-literary forms of criticism which were more appropriate to the work of the teachers in his audience than the methods and critical texts which derived from the canon of French literature. The theories which underpinned these new practices (materialist philosophies of various sorts, anthropological ideas of culture and myth, psycho-analytic theories of the self) had, by 1969, already begun to circumvent the more conservative writing of traditional literary critics.

By the end of the 60's, Barthes' third proposal – "at every opportunity and at every moment to develop the polysemic reading of the text"[105] – had already become a key element wherever university-educated writers took on board a radical agenda of critical and teaching practice. Perhaps this was often expressed as no more than a concern about relevance or about making connections with the contemporary world. With hindsight it can quickly be appreciated that a "polysemic" reading is a many-valued reading, a reading which allows for multiple meanings and for multiple styles of reading. Barthes wanted to propagate interlinked divergent readings of written texts – to *decompress* them, as he strikingly phrases it, through that multiplicity of readings. For Barthes the many-valued codes of sign systems call upon us in much the same way as the different but unacknowledged views and unheard voices of a colonised or repressed nation or a suppressed group or social class. Many-valuedness is, in other words, about being able to cross cultural frontiers. Here the concept of "reading" moves rapidly over into the construction of other forms of textuality, such as social reality for instance. What perhaps was not so readily understood by his contemporaries was the intensity, indeed the urgency, of Barthes' recommendation that this many-valuedness must, as he puts it, be searched for *at every opportunity, every moment:* it as if he is claiming that the search for multiple meaning is a positive duty of the critic. He extends the thought emphatically: we have to, he says, "recognise finally *the rights* of polysemy."[106]

***

Reflections on a Manual is as much an appraisal as it is a reaction to a historical moment. True, Barthes is writing in response to a time when there was, in every sense, a critical need to up-date writing-theory and literature-teaching. The then contemporary achievements in the human sciences, the impact of structuralist and post-structuralist theories in linguistics, the broad philosophical impact of quantum physics, the development of worldwide media and the emergence of popular culture all pointed in that direction. For Barthes there had occurred a "break" in modernity – a paradigm shift it might be called these days – which criticism and poetics had to take account of. But that said, Barthes' essay carefully and insightfully appraises the nature of reading in a quite literary way. Barthes' aim is to preserve the younger generation's access to the major writings of the past by linking them with contemporary reading practices.

Since Barthes' time no single public event – equivalent to *les événements* of Paris '68, that is – has fuelled the impetus behind a shift in critical thinking in the way that, arguably, the 1968 political and student movement did.

For Barthes' time, the new texts, the new arts and technologies, which undermined traditional curriculum could be related to disciplines within the human sciences –

---

105 Roland Barthes, op cit, p 28
106 Barthes, ibid. Italics added

anthropology, political economy, linguistics, structuralisms of various sorts, the study of mythology – and not just to external changes. At the same time, the development of a new "science" of semiotic reading involved a rethinking of literary study in relation to a prevalent, still widely respected contemporary teaching practice concerned with scholarly attentiveness to major historical examples defined within historically mapped genres. The shift was largely to do with how reading was done, how teaching was practised and what sorts of cultural object were deemed to be readable. Today, however, new pressures require a re-positioning of the practices of teaching and writing in relation to a philosophical area which, paradoxically, is itself still largely unknown and under-researched.

Today, the critique comes from areas which are largely technical, systems-oriented and practical, such as from information technology, from the instantanity of media and global communications and from a deep level of commodification at the heart of cultural practice. These changes do not arise from other disciplines in philosophy or in the arts. Further, what is being challenged is a traditional assumption which, unnoticeably, still operated at the heart of Barthes' approach. This assumption, quite defensible in the 1960s, was that, regardless of whether its figure is or is not that of the child absorbed in the book, the experience of recreative, critical reading remains the place on which critics and teachers should focus their attention. Whatever the new interconnections between text and writing, whatever the 1960s reader's immersion in cinema, TV and fashion, reading was how individuals accessed their world.

Readers, writers and critics are presently having to think themselves anew in relation to another *terra ignota*. This time it is not reading which is the key critical nexus but writing. It is not the adult reader who is the major aesthetic and critical territory of contention but the adult and young adult writer. Major components in the interrelations between text, voice, language, criticism, data and reading are changing in ways which appear to question historical truisms about writing, reading and text. Is the new reading page-based or hypertextual? Is writing now a mainly audio-visual form of scripting or a typographic form? Do texts any longer voice individual stylistic characteristics? What genres relate to interactive media and are any of them traditional literary genres? The answers to such questions extend beyond matters of genre. This is the point that Michael Heim makes when he says that the differences introduced by new reading and writing technologies cannot be satisfactorily explained within the terms only of what he calls a "switch in our epistemological stance". Just to think about reading in a different way does not really work. The changes occurring are to do with more than just how knowledge is represented or is accessed. Rather, those epistemological changes are changes in how we deal with information, store, access and memorise it. They are not just about the object of thought but about how we structure the very activity called "thinking". They are part of a deeply changing structure across the whole interface of thought and text and writing. Accordingly, they bring with them deep experiential shifts. For Heim it is a matter of an "ontological" shift in which there is "a change in the world under our feet, in the whole context in which our knowledge and awareness are rooted".[107]

Precise critical implications can easily be lost in endless enumerations of these new systems and in the complex, often highly rhetorical claims made about them. (The

---

107 Michael Heim, *The Metaphysics of Virtual Reality*, Oxford University Press, New York, 1993, p xiii

60s, too, were not exactly free of their own brand of utopian hype.) Nonetheless, I would claim that Barthes takes for granted that there is a close and productive symmetry between the four terms of teaching, literature, reception and readability. After all, how would you teach writing back in the 60s if not via a critical view of the literary tradition? How could literature be defined unless within ideas about teaching and reading? and are not criticism and teaching a key part of an informed discussion in which new writing (text, film, music, TV, fashion) can start to be received? This mutually supportive four-sided figure has to do with the formation of cultural meaning within a broad definition of the "contemporary" and with determining the way certain types of writing work – poetry, the novel, cartoon, script, captions and so on. Yet today in a manner which would perhaps surprise Barthes, the terms are ceasing to be mutually cohesive and there are indications of the ending of this pedagogical-literary system – and with it the demise of the very notions of text and textuality which are central to Barthes.

Teaching writing, the study of the text, an acknowledgement of the way multiple connections are made when reading – these activities have been modified and to some degree overtaken by the writing practices of the digital interface. A writing practice which, sampling and recombining from many different sorts of text and image, can then connect narratives in many-levelled networks is a writing which formally transcends the requirements of Barthes' notion of text. Interactivity, speed, access, multiple links, pathways – these are some features which determine writing in the hypertext domain. Barthes' readerly idea of polysemy and of acknowledging links between texts is far-sighted. But, however much it anticipates the structuring of writing as hypertext, it is an idea tied to the assumption that writing still represents a static, already completed cultural space bristling with signs to be analysed and essayed. It is all about reading and signifying and less about writing and interaction, less about captioning and connecting. Indeed a number of Barthes' favourite terms like "production" and "representation" now look too dated and metaphoric to pass without comment; they look, frankly, too doggedly *industrial* , "60s" in the bad sense. They derive too much from the workface and not enough from the interface.[108]

Reflections on a Manual was written in a period when it was still reasonable to assume a stability in the representational function of writing within the then technological context of publishing, of book writing and typefaces. Literature was a site, a representative zone, not least for political history and national identity. Barthes' view was that writing occurred as part of this so-called representational "space of language" mentioned earlier, a space occurring in the way thought is organised and the way a culture is sign-laden. Now we are encountering writing systems which are not representational in that sense at all. These new systems are, to borrow Gregory Ulmer's phrase, "chorographic":[109] they are not only writings within an already existent imaginary space of culture and communication but are themselves writings *of* space. These are writings which create space, fictively and cinematically, as well as in

---

108 The new interface is elaborated as much around practices of modality (of 'how to' and of 'how to get there') as around an idea of representation (i.e. here are the icons, here are the symbols); that is to say, it is built on the recognition that writing is a programming activity which programs not only the characteristics of texts but also the nature of human interactions with text. Theoretically, there are no productive/representational artifacts securely generated in the process of such writing even though what takes place is communication, exchange, design and data-management.
109 Gregory L. Ulmer, *Heuretics: The Logic of Invention*, The John Hopkins University Press, Baltimore, 1994, p 61 passim

who wants to create Australia?

terms of accessing already logged data. They build their own environment, their own environs, their own chora. Such writing at once involves the use of already constructed topographical systems i.e of networks and levels within data, but sometimes (as in CD-ROMs) also involves the literal building of such informational geographies anew. When accessed, these systems re-organise readability along the model of "journey" as a process of orientation, and they open up connectives between data, judgement, discovery and image which work in manifold, potentially many sided and linked ways.

In Barthes' sense of making a connection between teaching and literature, this sort of writing may have little or nothing to do with literary history or literary canons or aesthetic appreciation. Literature reduces within these chorographic systems to a database which can be sampled and downloaded as merely another sort of cultural information. The new interface seems, equally, to have little to do with the formation of a critically receptive "space" for judgement and appreciation. If anything, the space for reading has ceased to be a reflective space in the mind of an appreciative reader (that solitary reader with the book by the window) and has become an interactive, communicative space for which reading is the primary access code. Reading narrows functionally into being a point of entry for a viewer in front of a screen. True, the reader keeps on reading but not necessarily in a submerged, focussed way. Instead, passages of reading keep on offering new steps forward, new points of access.

There is also that matter of interlinkage between various sorts of reading. Barthes proposed a style of "polysemous" reading in which each textual instance is composed of a series of overlapping kinds of reading and in which each text can be placed in (and looked at from) different contexts. Examples such as operatic vocal style, the experience of playing music, the reading of a short story, the effect and affect of an advertisement could be read in relation to discourses of the body, discourses of popular entertainment, in relation to psychoanalysis, to media technologies, to mythic systems and so on. Barthes is somewhat like a narrowly trained professional of the text who suddenly wakes up one day and realises that there is a great deal more to see and talk about in the world than his strict discipline has led him to believe. The "decompression" he mentions is to do with breaking down boundaries and restrictions on what a reader and a critic can reference and happily the discipline of critical reading turns out to have multiple uses.

But things have moved on. The associative, so-called electronic logics of contemporary hypermedia and multimedia break out of these relativistic, many-sided notions of boundary. Links are made according to the productive possibilities of hyperlinkage – according to the design possibilities of "writing in" further and further links. True, all forms of generic distinctions between instances do not disappear: the modelling of a utopically constructed web of points floating in an infinitude of data remains a model which will always be restricted by actual uses. It is the case, nonetheless, that writing takes on the function of a design instrument which forms and follows linkages between points constructed as information centres (data banks, image repertoires, repertoires of sounds, moving images, interactive sites, live exchanges, live video-cams.) What is "decompressed" is not so much interpretation as any form of emphasis traditionally placed on differences of genre, differences of source and differences of context.

There is a claim even that such writing has a range and manoeuvrability across audio-visual regimes that move it close to dream work – to dream writing – and away from the powerful analogue established between written discourse and rational discourse which humanist teaching promotes. The electronic writing system is a writing system whose major impetus seems to be to give access to or to summon forth a "reading" which is more a form of reconnoitring than a form of linear decoding. Unlike reading traditionally conceived, the new practices are best defined as a highly active form of bricolage, a kind of bricolage in motion. Radically diverse types of discourse and information are rapidly flicked over via a form of reading and writing which patches things together, juxtaposing and intercutting broken up samples of texts. This difference in logic between conventional script systems and hyperlink systems, says Gregory Ulmer, is "the point of departure for imagining what a new rhetoric will do that does not argue but that replaces the logic governing argumentative writing with associational networks."[110] In short, even the interconnection between the representative space of humanist writing and of dialectical, argumentative logic is wearing thin. We are encountering, as Ulmer says elsewhere, a writing which is paradoxically beyond representation or "the other side of rhetoric".

***

Might it not be the case that, precisely in the light of these new interfacial, consciously modal ways of writing, it is urgent that there remains a place not just for, but *of*, writing. This will be a place which encapsulates a feature of writing which Barthes hardly touches on in his essay: creativity, the creative impulse in literary writing, and the deep poetic interlinkages between language and experience. The nexus between teaching and text is no longer one which establishes the symbiosis of teaching with literature. Teaching "text" has become, as we oberve in many schools and universities, an activity to do with planning access to the informational system and perhaps (at best) about encouraging creative writing in media-associated "old style" genres such as fiction. Multimedia design, hyper-rhetoric, the creation of interactive systems, the capacity to access data – these become core elements in a teaching practice which is addressed less to interpretation than to writing, imagining, designing and thinking. Whereas Barthes felt it essential to maintain what he termed the antinomy between literary practice and literary teaching – in other words, felt it essential to divide the notion of writing into the two parts of the creative and the teacherly – it could be the case that the distinction cannot come into play in interface systems. It is not necessarily to damn the new media to recognise that critical and historical depth of understanding and the capacity to refine judgement seem to have only a small place in electronic writing. It is merely to acknowledge how far writing is becoming dislocated from these traditional contextual practices in literary criticism and judgement.

Yet that other profound difficulty which Barthes mentioned, the problem of transmitting knowledge, does not go away even if we cannot any longer divide off (as Barthes does) critical practice from creative engagement. Here it could be argued that all transmissive systems – in media and in art no less than in knowledge disciplines – currently face a moment of crisis deeper than the issue of a modern "break" which faced the school teachers back in 1969. For Barthes, this problem of knowledge was a problem

---

110 Gregory L. Ulmer, op cit, p 18

identified under the name of alienation – in other words, a problem of relevance, of how to make literature applicable to the young, of the connectedness of literature, philosophy and art to the TV generation, to the post-structuralist generation. It was about how to make an adjustment, how to accommodate the contemporary world.

For us, the problem of knowledge is perhaps more severe. On the one hand the problem concerns the status of knowledge (is it more than data? what is new knowledge? and how is it to be researched and debated?) And as in Barthes' day it still concerns the matter of relevance and need (do we any longer need to undergo the slow process of acquiring disciplinary knowledges?) But much more than just a "break" with modernity, this question is now a question to do with the maintenance of skilled, deeply informed, authoritative, creative practice in writing. Fundamentally, what *is* creative literature in the age of cybernetics? Is there any room for it, any need for it? In the open-ended system of bricolage, what determines the nature of creative and recreative utterance? Our children do not sit by the kitchen stove reading the classics voraciously while tea is being prepared – and have not done so for at least two generations. They are not out in the backyard under the mulberry tree reading Faulkner or Pound and they may well never get to hear of the Milton who is not a cartoon character but a poet. They are looking at screens, checking in to chat rooms, accessing web pages, web logging, data sharing, or watching TV and videos. These are the foundational childhood activities into which the experience of literature has somehow to fit.

Thinking about language, meaning and imagination cannot be separated out from writing. Of course such a statement looks like a steep cliff wall of a generalisation: yet, in everyday fact, it is obviously the case that some deployment or testing out of what we mean by communication, by making sense and by imaginative projection on the world around us is always at stake when we write. This is true even of the note left on the kitchen table – with its promises about back in half an hour or its historical projection of "In town to do the shopping." To study the connection between the main aspects of creative practice (language, meaning, imagination, writing) is central to the study of poetics and might remain at the heart of any contemporary practice to do with teaching language and writing. Poetics, however, is not proposed here as a substitute foundational discipline, nor as the sort of extended heuristic method which semiotics was for Barthes. Poetics is both speculative and practical: it is *both* a study of the way in which knowing is represented *and* a doing of that knowledge. Traditionally conceived disciplinary outcomes, it is true, may not apply here: a large part of poetics is not just a study about a modality of experience but a shaping and making conscious of experience. Often the idea of experience will include areas of emotional response difficult to name and threshold senses of things. Besides, to write, to imagine, to think is to study the nature of the dream no less than the nature of a conscious determination of a "what is".

Of course, there are special conditions and limits which thread through various aspects of the contemporary interface, emphasising – and to a degree, over-emphasising and therefore distorting – the way in which writing, sound and visual image interact. This is a period, for instance, where audio-visual and televisual means of communicating and representing have an enormous physical reach and psychological presence; but will this always be the case and will not current audio-visual forms keep on changing? Poetics is the area in which truth-conditions – questions about illusion, reality and the mediating function of language – can be explored and understood. Accordingly, another way of defining poetics might be as a study which comprises in the broadest sense a metaphorics, a discourse on, and analysis of, the work of metaphor. This metaphorics can be conducted through a variety of areas of study whether literary, psychoanalytic, cinematic, philosophical, systemic, cognitive or ecological. But a no less relevant way of defining poetics might be as a study which explores the immersion of each individual in his or her own metaphoric construction of the world. The study of poetics is, in this sense, a study of what might be termed "realisation". It is about bringing to consciousness one's own and one's work's relationship with its setting, with its time whether in the large sense of period or the more immediate sense of biographical experience.

To study and practise poetics, to engage with writing's creative practices, is to address a complex, overlaid space where a multiplicity of experiences merge, start, stop, appear and disappear. It is a space much like a phenomenologist might describe it – dependent on the relationship of things to context, shifting and changing and integrated with lived, human experiences of it. Writing has always been an activity not just about invention from experience but also about exploring and shaping the ontological status of experience. Yet at the same time, writing is the key to the range of reflective practices on which the concepts of "analysis" and "reflection" are based. A poetics of writing articulates a space necessary for interrupting what threatens to be a seamless relationship between managerialism and massively technological, over-realised determinations of the interface; it will energise a writing which risks being numbed by its use as a merely political instrument.

4

In still pools stones
Have the clarity
Of eggs in a nest.
They lie like thoughts in the mind.

David Campbell

country and how to get there

*M*y idea of Australia changed when I bought a few acres of it. To be precise, I bought four acres and a nearly completed house. The property is a couple of hours outside Sydney in a winding valley surrounded by paddocks set among national park and state forests.

The house has power, and therefore phone, fax, internet and e-mail, but no town water. TV reception is rare and ABC radio offers clear moments among real storms and the blurring which has recently resulted from Liberal and National Party control and interference. The house's location is deceptive for, despite its relative wildness, the valley is one of the earliest colonially settled areas outside Sydney. Mostly graziers searching out runs for cattle, Europeans arrived in the late 1820s and early 1830s. There is still evidence of those early inhabitants: for instance, a few remaining convict-hewn sandstone houses. The quickly superseded Great North Road built by prisoner chaingangs in the 1830s is a couple of paddocks away from my fence line. There are literary remains too. The valley was home to Eliza Dunlop, a 19th century poet and song writer. From an upstairs window I can see a mile or so across the valley to the sandstone house where theologian and anthropologist, Elkin, lived in the 1920s. More recent memory, however, has set out very few claims to fame. From the 50s on, the place drifted into being a cut-off backwater kept going by a handful of dairy farmers. As the value of the dairy subsidy fluctuated and declined, the tree line slowly crept down the slopes and barns and slab huts fell into disrepair.

This orchard acreage was clearly something of an experiment. I had moved up and down Australia getting to know the country relatively well, driving and flying whether for conferences or radio work or just travelling around and sight seeing. I am anyway probably someone inclined to focus on the unbuilt environment, not least through the influence of childhood memory. The natural environment and its connection with the built environment have remained important to me as a source of reflection and engagement, and inevitably therefore of subject matter. In terms of metaphor and immediate senses of place, some of my poems take up the themes of paddocks and fences and orchards and hillsides.

The fact was, though, that since my early twenties I had not made any serious attempt at living outside the city. Moving to the valley I had a private and hopefully not too pretentious aim which I was nearly prepared to admit to myself: whatever the outcome, I wanted to check out, renew and explore immediate senses of what can all too loosely be called "local", a sense of "place" or Australia's "natural environment". Perhaps there would be an adjustment to a lop-sided sense of the broader cultural as well as sensory environment. This experiment too was to do with knowing something about not being on the coast, about being closer to a more detailed sense of the drier inland environment which many Australians are hesitant about. Again I hope it is not too extravagant to say that in my own mind it was a matter of knowing something more about natural proportions at work in that non-coastal environment, between ways to live and a sense of locale.

So I had just moved to the country? In Australia, "country" is not about a settled patchwork landscape of towns and farms. Besides, only the immediate coastal hinterland of South Eastern Australia resembles that sort of physical and human geography – and even there many places do not. Instead, the local use of the word country mostly lacks the definite article "the" and (to repeat a phrase used elsewhere in this book) is technical, intimate and surprisingly mystical. You can own country, you can lament it, you can feel attached to it, you can hate it, you can see it being degraded or cared for, you can feel that it is yours in a blood sense. But to be living "in the country" in the sense of being in the countryside, though definitely an alloweable useage, remains a somewhat European usage. "In the country" is a phrase more apposite to a 19th century novelist like Turgenev where the student children return to the parents' country estate or it might apply to the division between town and country in a place like Britain.

Australian "country" is less like the countryside which some Europeans tried to invent in 19th century Australia than a new sort of amalgam derived from different pastoral uses of land plus the effect of non-European climatic conditions on the productivity of land. The relative absence of population is a factor too as are the influence of Aboriginal land practices and Aboriginal ancestral senses of custodianship. This continuing Indigenous influence is often underacknowledged. "Country", accordingly, references many sorts of terrain, whether a parcel of land or a huge stretch driven through for days on end; while, on other occasions, it is a term closer in meaning to the sense of a birthright area or a home area. The word's use oscillates all the way between how an Indigenous Australian might use it to describe where he or she comes from through to the self consciously academic adoption of the term as a tool to shift perceptions of ownership, care and environment within the larger geopolitical terrain of national life and ideas. "Country" is a word which upsets the neat overlaps of meaning in terms like "land", "property", "farm", "home", "district", "landscape", separating these meanings out from each other and stressing how each brings with it its own slant of non-Indigenous colonial history.

Some of the issues involved, mainly of land and identity, are amongst modern Australian poetry's core issues, articulating a matter deeply set in the national psyche: the question of what sort of poetry typifies "our" idea of local experience. In the worst case, it is true that some writers prefer to take the round-the-world ticket route to universality, writing poetry which looks as though it has been written anywhere where American TV is staple diet. But really, recent Australian poetry has no more and no less of this featureless worldspeak than the rest of the English speaking world's contemporary poetries have. However, what constitutes the opposite of this blandness – one of the options being the representation of local aspects of voice and tone – is far from clear. Whilst there is an almost knee-jerk tendency to refer to the rural voice as somehow obviously distinctive, it is too easy and too reductive to take it as the wider community's touchstone. Is this rural voice a more foundational poetic voice than any other? Why should it be? And, besides, is there only one country voice, and by extension only one national voice? The truth is that poetic voice is not reducible to a regional consideration or a sociological descriptor. Judith Wright, for example, wrote poetry of the land more profound than any of her contemporaries, but in most ways her poetry speaks largely without regional tonal inflection. Inflection is not what makes it Australian.

It is a truism, of course, to say that poetic voice is more than a matter of colloquial phrasing. No less crucial to poetry is its capacity to identify sensorily, and in that sense to localise, what we have always noticed but never consciously seen, heard and felt. In memorable poems, names occur for what has familiarly pressed upon the viewer or listener in a manner seemingly between names or on the edge of language. More than voice, this ability to find the right word is why, at its most pleasurable, poetry maintains a natural access to what is local, what is specific and striking. Good poetry keeps the channels with the local world open, flowing and fresh. Likewise, we at once know that something is going wrong in a poem as soon as we sense that the project, the scope of imagining, the way things are placed in the poem, are detached from a living context of experience. This is most obvious when, for instance, the themes and styles of a particular poet's work are generated only from what might be termed the repertoire of good ideas, framed with an obligatory sense of what the proper theme for a poem is. Recently that has tended to mean a poetry originated from the debris of various earlier kinds of modernism whether surrealisms of various sorts or the mannerisms of late modernist American poetry or the generalised pressure in post-modern poetry towards de-referenced language. Shards and fragments of various 20th century literary movements, sometimes these borrowed flashes of modernity can still bring their moments of fire and insight. Yet the ease with which they can thoughtlessly be made use of can delude the writer into believing that clever, look-alike, derivative poems somehow substitute for the real thing.

The line or phrase which breaks through like a suddenly recognisable signal is the one where the thing and the space it is in quickly and brilliantly merge in the eye and on the ear. This moment of convergence, a moment where things at last fit appropriately into their environment, often occurs seamlessly and as if it has always been the way to name and see. The fineness of many of Les Murray's poems, for instance, is often to do with such moments. Sometimes these places of convergence occur in images carefully pointed up in a way which highlights their newness; at other times, convergence occurs with an utter naturalness of phrase. One of Murray's many definitions of "sprawl," for instance, in his poem "The Quality of Sprawl" demonstrates this natural, understated manner in which Murray seems effortlessly to get things right. "Sprawl," he writes,

is doing your farming by aeroplane, roughly…[111]

The phrase perfectly and humorously defines a particular Australian perception of how to connect up outback immensity *and* practicality. How else could you farm other than by plane? But it does so in a line nearly offhand in delivery and calculatedly indifferent to the sheer extravagance of the idea: this is what produces the comic effect of the tacked-on word "roughly".

---

111 Les Murray, op cit, p 182

In other examples, however, Murray highlights the effect more deliberately, letting us know that he is conscious of the specificity (and newness) of what he is seeing. Thus for instance, the well-known opening of "The Flying-Fox Dreaming, Wingham Brush, New South Wales" with its reference to the way evening light, spread along the landscape's flat ridges, seems to filter sideways through open-limbed eucalypts:

> ...the west
> is lighting in under the leaves
> and Hookfoot the eagle
> has gone from over the forest....[112]

A reader can immediately sense the flickering effect of the light, a flickering effect carried by the deliberately cumbersome phrase "lighting in under". Something is said here in a moment of visual and emotional convergence in a way which is deft and unforgettably local. If you have seen this common feature of Australian dusk light you know that Murray's poem speaks it completely.

In other places, it is as if his metaphor is like someone watching, taking time to focus, squint, size up and take in the object. When reading this last sort of line the reader will think, re-think and then assess the aptness of the phrasing. The reader consciously needs time to see a newly defined phenomenon freshly. The opening line of "Equanimity" is a good example of this delaying tactic or focussing device. Here the poem starts off with the line:

> Nests of golden porridge shattered in the silky-oak trees...[113]

It takes a while longer to gauge how Murray is identifying the deep orange burnish of these native trees' flower sprays. Anyone who has seen them knows that the flowers sit in layered clusters in the tree and they do not produce elegant spired flowers or rich mists of blooms. But are they "porridge" exactly? The phrase "golden porridge" is both shocking and insightful. Indeed silky-oaks form thick, irregular, randomly scattered clusters (arguably, like nests) of orange-brown, sometimes almost bark-coloured flowers. Yet the "porridge" effect with its trace of splatter inevitably stays in the mind. It tells you that Murray is looking at the silky oaks from some distance for when seen individually the silky-oak flower is not porridge-like but a finely formed grevillea-like spray. In one and the same moment, the image reveals both the tentativeness, the closeness, the distance and then the security with which the poet's focus realises these unconventionally beautiful flowers.

Murray's poems often have this ability to size up and then think through a moment of perception, extending what he sees and how he senses into the image's naming-game as if the process of seeing and feeling is naturally contoured by the thing and not only by thought. In "Grassfire Stanzas", he describes how the paddocks get burnt off in late winter, leaving "black centres" expanding on the afternoon paddock. Already everything in that phrase about expanding black centres bespeaks the winter light, the airy immensity of the paddock slopes, the softening light falling on grey-blond dry grass. Then he goes on:

---

112 Les A. Murray, *Ethnic Radio*, Angus and Robertson, Sydney, 1977, p 3 where the poem appears with this title, shortened in other collections of the poems
113 Les Murray, 2002, op cit, p 178

> The blackenings are balanced, on a gradient of dryness
> in the almost-still air, between dying thinly away
> and stripping the whole countryside. Joining, they never gain
> more than they lose. They spread away from their high moments.[114]

The effect is magical. The reader can watch the movement of fire across ground as if it is a perfect emanation of balance and re-composure, as if indeed there is a physical internalisation of upsurge and rejoining in the motion of these low barriers of flames.

This ability to gauge the intuitive connections between thought and object argues a capacity in poetry which is not only about defining a lived sense of locale but a capacity to capture a play of natural proportions between things and their environment. Murray works with that knowledge abundantly. Other poets have this gift too. Nor is it restricted to examples where "particulars" (flames, flowers, crop dusting or helicopter mustering) are the objects of attention. This same gift can be found in contexts where very large things are in focus or indeed where focus gives way to a blending of foreground and background or to a sense of movement and change. This natural relatedness is found, for instance, in poetry where suddenly the relatedness between what are immeasurable dimensions – and, in particular, dimensions influenced by entirely personal senses of the world – are caught in a series of poetic interconnections.

This is what occurs in David Campbell's account of the relation between train tracks and the skyline in "The Wimmera":

> Steel lines melt
> Into the rim of the horizon
> Where plain and sky are welded
> And at intervals shimmer
> Along the tracks like bins
> The silver temples of Ceres
> In whose shadow tractors crawl
> Over the floor of the plain
> As mortal as men
> Before the vast seasons
> Brown green and blond...[115]

Seen at different levels of closeness and farness many objects criss-cross and merge here. What surrounds these small townships with their metal-roofed houses and their gleaming wheat silos is a mobile impression of immensely open flat country. Campbell's poem maintains a set of immeasurable relations between height and width, between smallness and largeness, treating them as elements which are vectoring relatively to each other, as indeed they do when you are crossing such flat country by train or car. Here, utterance and seeing have such an intuitive join between them that it is not just a place (a silo, a township) which holds in the mind's eye but a whole modality of being in, and moving in, this inland place. The effect is cinematic, more like shooting a video than looking at a single photograph.

Inland places perhaps allow for these mobile relationships between height and depth because of the inland's spaciousness. Hills, valleys and forests do not get in the way. Philip Hodgins captures a more static, a more purely photographic version of

---

114 Murray, op cit, p 163

115 David Campbell, "The Wimmera", *Collected Poems* ed. Leonie Kramer, Angus and Robertson, Sydney, 1989, p 294

this spacious, immeasurable quality of empty sky and height and distance in "A Note from Mindi Station". Under this inland skyscape, he writes of how isolation can seem quite "reasonable" and how in that space

> ...a sparrow hawk was hovering there.
> Its legs had been let down with claws outstretched,
> the wings had worked themselves into a blur,
> the head was changing settings like a switch;
> but what was fixed in place was one small bird
> which might have been the pivot of the world...[116]

What intuitively links perception with its natural context is not only a sense of geometry in the bird's hovering but also an intensely felt identification with height and aerial viewpoint, with hanging in the air like that sparrow hawk. Which way do height and depth pivot here? Hodgins seems able to look up at the hawk, and at the same time, down across the land from the bird's position.

Other Australian poets take this physical sense of experience into a more self reflexive idea about how poetic imagery and language can work. Jennifer Rankin comes to mind again (as she often does when I think about poems which explore space) especially for her poems about what she calls "the line" and her poems about flying. These poems are preoccupied with the experience of earth and with horizontal shapes. Being a true poet, she knew many painters, a companionable fact which no doubt influenced her poetry's technical range and its identification with the flat pictorial space of then contemporary abstract and abstract-expressionist painting. Reading her, it is as if she is searching towards a literary accommodation of how that type of Australian painting adopts, and then changes, flat abstract and minimalist surfaces into a particularly appropriate way of seeing Australia. Flat-surface abstract painting becomes, in effect, a non-abstract "realism". These revisions of late modernist pictorial space open a way to observe grain, texture and the minuteness of things when dwarfed by the air. Rankin's poems similarly draw our attention to the minutiae of natural phenomena and to the need to find names for visual and auditory effects which otherwise remain unconscious and namelessly abstract influences. She lets us see what is at the edge of vision.

Was moving away from the city my own way of encouraging some such intuitive influences of time, land form and season to be at work on my sense of the world around me? Of course, the processes of poetry are paradoxical and cannot be willed even by the best of designs. For what is at issue in a poem is not just the intention to see things newly but rather the ability to accept and find words for convergences and connections which seem to hover on the edge of understanding. The place where I am writing this essay, for instance, appears at first sight to be a place in nature, in the wilderness, in the bush. Once you know about it, however, you do not forget how several hundred metres away is that fence-line of one of surveyor Mitchell's early 19th century projects, the Great North Road. Given that the road placed a European structure and a European concept of travel across this country, you could even say that it was the road which brought wilderness to this place, for it brought what we mean by the concept of untravelled country. It set wildness and impenetrability apart

---

116 Philip Hodgins, "A Note from Mindi Station", *New Selected Poems*, Duffy and Snellgrove, Sydney 2000, p 12

from, and at each side of, the culverts and bridges and stone paved embankments of an early 19th century European road. By the same token, once you understand how quickly the road was rendered technically unnecessary by the colony's rapid development of steamship travel and telegraph communication, the road instantly gets associated with that common feature of colonial Australia: futility and unpredictability in assuming that you can plan and map out the future. Perhaps the road assisted the first influx of wheat farmers with road transport for a few years but their farms are long gone: mostly, their buildings were wooden and insubstantial and wheat is a not a crop grown here for a century or more. The truth is that the appearance of the land here has been utterly transformed by clearance, by farming, by regrowth, by abandoned house sites, by floods. The small, shallow lake which the house looks over had one of the largest flour-mills outside of Sydney on its shores. If you search you find that there are a few scattered bricks where perhaps it once stood. Other than that, no foundation stone, no platform or earth terrace mark its location now.

The fact of so much already non-existent, so much already vanished, could suggest that country inevitably demands that we understand the relationship between openness, wilderness, habitation and travel as a series of transformative experiences of place, both across time and through multiple senses of environment and place. Even the most deeply and intuitively acquired senses of time, land form and weather cannot help but be historical. Here history might mean recognising detailed micro-structures of recurrence and variation in rain or seasonal drought or animal and bird movement as well as what we normally expect it to mean: huge decade-long climatic movements or lifelong human uses and shapings of country. This, in part, is why the Aboriginal story teller has told us that we must dig deeper than the white soil of the surface and try to find the black soil inside it. "You been diggin only white soil..." is how this old man put it. Even the multiple layering and transformation of European settlement is, in this sense, not much deeper than white soil.

Back in the valley, for instance, it takes a while before you understand one of its most obvious features: the convergence of two part-flowing creeks next to a patch of water, a sort of soak, folded into the hills. It is a kind of lake or large pond, but no-one normally calls it by either of those names. It would be uncomfortable and perhaps pedantic to do so. No-one knows what the lived and dreamt connection with this water place has been; nor with its surrounding arms and valley sides or with the further reaches of the valley, its escarpments and rock shelves. Of course once you look, the whole geographical area, covering hundred and hundred of hectares, is dotted with paintings and rock carvings. There are so many that you would have to be someone whose view of history was so populist and repressively right wing that you could not accept reflecting on the dispossession and so-called dispersal which occurred here when permanent settlement and farming took on. The most obvious features of this place such as the natural contours of land, the abundance of birds and wallabies, the junction of two part-flowing creeks, the permanent shallow soak suggest focus and residence. Of course this richly-inhabited place is where the original small settler township was surveyed and built.

To understand the connectedness of human presence across time goes to the heart of that matter of how the words "country" and "land" and "countryside" connect up. In city people this knowledge of prior Aboriginal residency can readily inspire constructive action mixed with guilt, whereas a mixture of fellow feeling, resignation and responsibility is a much more likely emotion in country areas. Spoken or unspoken, these shadings of perception contribute to the fact that, whether they weekend or run tax write-off cattle or farm for a living or have working vineyards, many (not all) of my neighbours see their tenure as temporary and, by their own lights, custodial. Arguably, too much has already happened in this utterly still, sometimes sky-drowned bit of country. Even Aboriginal historical presence can no longer by itself identify the full shape of the remembering here, no matter how much Aboriginal absence creates the play of terms, the dimensions of feeling, the endless repeatings and no less regular memory failures which build the deepest context by which this place is a place.

Like everywhere in Australia, this patch of country is a surface which, studied closely, has been lived in again and again. Of course, modern poems cannot be required to be only about re-creating location. Yet a surprisingly large number of Australian poems address the issue of place whether that sense of location is conceived as a place in language and idiom or in the mind or as an actual humanly loved, family-lived place which the writer captures. In such poems what emerge are dazzling and utterly convincing leaps of thought best done when the images offer moments of convergence, insight and sensation. Because these poems are places where energies of mind, eye, ear and body converge, these moments do not reduce to being only about things, places, sensations and visions in an obvious descriptive way, as if somehow the "thing" is achieved and the imaging and telling terminable. No moment is ever finally got right, in that way. It has to be told and re-told in order to live, in order to be restored to us; which is probably one reason why significant writers return and return to the same themes and images throughout a lifetime's work. For some such ability to capture contemporary ways of seeing and travelling in country is a key activity. It is how, expertly drawn into the fabric of language and imagination, country enters into unconscious and intuitive areas of the mind.

index

Also available from
HALSTEAD PRESS

A.D. HOPE: SELECTED POETRY & PROSE
The best and most characteristic of a lifetime's work. Hope's classical approach to verse form, his unblushing exploration of erotic themes, his lucid and striking images are all richly paraded. 240 pages

LOOSE LIPS, *with a foreword by Martin Harrison*
An exciting collection of fiction, poetry and reflections from candid new Australian writers tipped to be the big names of tomorrow. 192 pages

WAR IN WORDS; THE HALSTEAD ARMOURY OF AUSTRALIAN WAR WRITING *edited by Matthew Richardson.*
Foreword by Gen. Peter Cosgrove.
From Furphy's sardonic tale of the 1856 Arrow War, to post-Vietnam reflections on the aftermath of conflict: a striking array of poetry and prose. 272 pages

REAL RELATIONS *by Susan Lever*
Examines a century of Australian realist writing, challenging the assumption that it speaks for patriarchal liberalism. In authors like Henry Handel Richardson, Furphy, Patrick White and Sally Morgan, Lever finds new insight on gender and literary form. 176 pages

THE WRITER'S READER *edited by Brenda Walker*
Leading Australian writers explain how its done—Deb Westbury on poetic metaphor, Stephen Muecke on fictocriticism, Glenda Adams on voice, and many others. 208 pages

FACE TO FACE (*Southerly* 63/2)
A volume of discussions with Australian poets, new poetry, reviews and essays—available singly through bookstores, or by subscribing to *Southerly*. 224 pages

BOXKITE
Australia's international journal of writing and poetics sets the highest standards in presentation of cutting edge poetry and criticism. Double issue 3/4 (432 pages) features Charles Olsen, Tanikawa, Rimbaud and a supplement on Japan. In bookshops and on subscription.

HALSTEAD PRESS
300/3 Smail St, Broadway, NSW, 2007
Tel: 02 9211 3033 Fax: 02 9211 3677 Email: halstead@halsteadpress.com.au

SYDNEY MMIV
Published by Halstead Press
300/3 Smail Street,
Broadway, New South Wales, 2007

National Library cataloguing-in-publication entry

Harrison, Martin, 1949–.
Who wants to create Australia? : essays on poetry and ideas in contemporary Australia.

Includes index.
ISBN 1 920831 20 7

1. Australian poetry – 21st century – History and
   criticism.
I. Title.

A821.4